The World's
Greatest Psychics

The World's Greatest Psychics

Nostradamus to John Edward, Predictions
and Prophecies, Hits and Misses

Francine Hornberger

CITADEL PRESS
Kensington Publishing Corp.
www.kensingtonbooks.com

CITADEL PRESS BOOKS are published by

Kensington Publishing Corp.
850 Third Avenue
New York, NY 10022

Copyright © 2004 Francine Hornberger

All Kensington titles, imprints, and distributed lines are available at special quantity discounts for bulk purchases for sales promotions, premiums, fund-raising, educational, or institutional use. Special book excerpts or customized printings can also be created to fit specific needs. For details, write or phone the office of the Kensington special sales manager: Kensington Publishing Corp., 850 Third Avenue, New York, NY 10022, attn: Special Sales Department; phone 1-800-221-2647.

CITADEL PRESS and the Citadel logo are Reg. U.S. Pat. & TM Off.

First printing: November 2004

10 9 8 7 6 5 4 3 2 1

Printed in the United States of America

Library of Congress Control Number: 2004106179

ISBN 0-8065-2615-7

To Christopher, for all that he makes possible

Contents

Acknowledgments	ix	Jeane Dixon	86
Introduction	1	John Edward	91
		Maria Esperanza	96
Dorothy Allison	7	The Fatima Seers	103
Rosemary Altea	11	Sonya Fitzpatrick	109
George Anderson	16	Leslie Flint	114
Apollonius of Tyana	19	The Fox Sisters	120
Biblical Prophets	25	Uri Geller	129
Elijah	26	George Ivanovitch	
Isaiah	28	Gurdjieff	134
Amos	28	Craig and Jane	
Jonah	29	Hamilton-Parker	139
Ezekiel	30	John Holland	143
Jeremiah	31	Daniel Dunglas Home	147
Daniel the Prophet	31	Peter Hurkos	153
John the Baptist	33	Elizabeth Joyce	157
St. John the Divine	34	The Amazing Kreskin	161
Helena Petrovna Blavatsky	35	Margery the Medium	165
William Branham	41	Wolf Messing	173
Dannion Brinkley	46	Ruth Montgomery	175
Sylvia Browne	52	Nostradamus	183
Count Alesandro		Eusapia Palladino	189
di Cagliostro	57	Grigori Rasputin	193
Edgar Cayce	61	Mother Shipton	199
Aleister Crowley	69	Emanuel Swedenborg	202
Andrew Jackson Davis	75	James van Praagh	211
John Dee	79		
The Delphic Oracle	82	*Sources*	217

Acknowledgments

On a book, it's the author's name that appears on the cover, but credit belongs to many. For the most part, a writer works in isolation. However, those who exist outside that self-imposed Siberia make sure things happen while the writer taps away on the keys and deserve much gratitude and respect.

First and foremost, my heartfelt thanks goes to the esteemed Margaret Wolf, who pushed to get this book signed, and to Bruce Bender, who graciously relented. Amanda Rouse took over the reigns, and with amazing patience and professionalism, and Miles Lott took it to the finish line. And I could never forget my research assistants, without whom any writer might literally die. Christine Guarino Mayer and Derek Hornberger helped me find information that was interesting, salient, and obscure, which is the most difficult task, especially in such a saturated subject.

Many thanks go to the psychics and psychic organizations who so generously shared photos and information with me.

Barry Manilow, Donna Summer, Julie Andrews, and the soundtracks of several Broadway productions also need to be wholeheartedly thanked—but let's leave it at that. And while I'm on this track, thanks must also be given to Fluffy, Casey, Spike, and Annie. Their unbelievable cuteness provided much-needed, however well-rued, procrastination breaks.

Special mention goes out to the people in my personal and professional life who have tolerated me through the completion of this project. Thank you to my family, friends, and colleagues who have, by now, learned to put up with my countless absences and absentmindedness, flakiness and forgetfulness, crankiness and cancellations, as I worked through getting the darn thing done, and who always somehow manage to muster much unrelenting patience and support. This goes especially for Christopher LaSala, who has essentially taken

Acknowledgments

over the role of "bride" in planning our upcoming wedding, while I have plowed through the writing of this book. He, more than anyone, fully realizes what it means to actually live with a writer, and he has chosen to spend his life with me anyway.

The World's Greatest Psychics

Introduction

The *New Age A to Z* defines a psychic as someone "who is born with or develops many gifts in the area of ESP, clairvoyance, communication with the spirit world, abilities to read the human aura and uses these special skills as a healer or reader." Yes, the range is broad, but essentially a psychic is a person whose sixth sense is as well developed as his or her other senses, and who relies on this sense just as unconsciously and just as regularly. It describes a person who presumes to see, feel, and do things that ordinary five-sensed folks just can't.

Being a psychic does not always mean you can tell the future, that you can see and communicate with the dead, that you communicate directly with God, that you can bend flatware with your mind, or that you make things materialize and disappear. Just as with any other profession or vocation, there are many areas of specialty. While some may purport to have more than one extrasensory gift, most focus on and develop just one.

Psychics have been known by many names, depending on these specialties. They have been called soothsayers, oracles, prophets, mediums, clairvoyants, mind readers, fortune-tellers, and telepaths, and, on the other end of the spectrum, charlatans, frauds, exploiters, tricksters, and even heretics. Throughout time, people have been fascinated by psychics, whether because they buy into them hook, line, and—some may say—sucker, or because they have devoted their careers, lo their lives, to picking up inconsistencies and showing up fraudulence and fakery.

But like them or not, believe in them or don't, psychics have flourished and thrived since the dawn of time, despite the some-times-seething reproof of skeptics—and even despite the fact that what they perceive and communicate and actually do is not usually ever wholly accurate or believable. Through it all, psychics have been revered and reviled in every culture, both in the Eastern world and in the less-tolerant-of-intangibles West.

Some don't want to acknowledge how closely intertwined are the concepts of religion and extrasensory perception. But think about it: Both require a belief past what is known and what can be seen—an extension of belief past what is tangible—and belief in either can, at times, be met with the chuckles and disdain of nonbelievers. Both can be misleading, but at the core, the existence of both is based entirely on faith.

Ironically, many religions—Christianity especially—denounce the idea of "psychic powers." However, in special cases, there have even been popes who have accepted psychic ability—to a point. The Bible is full of psychics and supernatural tales. Visions from the heavens and predictions of events to come can be found in its pages. That said, the "major religious prophets," like Moses, Jesus, and Mohammed, have not been included in this collection; however, other religious figures—prophets, seers, and mystics—have.

Many famous people have been entranced and enchanted by the possibility of psychic power. Sherlock Holmes creator Arthur Conan Doyle devoted a huge part of his career providing psychic validity, even risking and losing friends and, in large part, reputation. His association with the King of all Skeptics, Harry Houdini, was especially volatile. They had, at one time, been friends—that is, until Doyle tried to convince Houdini that he had a letter from Houdini's mother, Cecilia Weiss, from beyond the grave; that the letter was not in Houdini's native Hungarian (Weiss spoke no English), and that his mother seemed not to know it was her own birthday, caused Houdini to essentially write off Doyle for good. Doyle's faith never waned, however. Before he died, he wrote, "The reader will judge that I have had many adventures. The greatest and most glorious of all awaits me now."

Also in strong support of many psychics, but not all, were the husband-and-wife romance poets, the Brownings, as well as many other writers. In the modern era, Shirley MacLaine shocked many— and converted many more—with her belief in reincarnation and past lives. Even First Lady Nancy Reagan called on psychics, such as Jeane Dixon (see page 86), to plot her and her husband's charts. But these are just a few of the many.

Of course, skeptics abound. For every person who believes, there are at least two who don't. Interestingly enough, the most vehement opponents of psychics, next to scientists, are magicians and illusionists. While they also push the limits of believability through the all-important "wow factor," their gripe is that while they are amazing folks with sleight of hand, it's out in the open that they are creating illusions: For the illusionists, it's like the devil you know and the devil you don't.

Houdini was at once one of the greatest magicians and steadfast skeptics of all time. He wasn't always skeptical, however. He used to want to believe it was possible to communicate with the other side, especially after his mother died in 1913, an event he described as "a shock from which I do not believe recovery is possible." Houdini trudged from medium to medium trying to find one who could help him communicate with his mother, but he never felt anything but exploited by them. He soon thought all mediums were all fakes, and hence devoted his life to discrediting them—in droves. Houdini liked to attend séances in disguise, scrutinizing the events without anyone paying attention to what he was doing. When he saw the trick the false medium was using, he would pull off his false beard, glasses, or wig—whatever he happened to be using to conceal his true identity—stand up, and gleefully gloat, "I am Houdini! And you are a fraud!"

Randall James Hamilton Zwinge, more commonly known as James Randi and, even more commonly, as "the Amazing Randi," is to this era what Houdini was to his. (Believers in reincarnation may raise an eyebrow at the fact that Randi was born in 1928, less than two years after Houdini's death.) Randi says that people buy into psychic phenomenon because "people want control over their lives. And they want some magic." This magician, clearly, isn't *looking* for magic, at least not that variety. So convinced is Randi that psychic phenomenon is an unsubstantial pseudoscience, his foundation, the James Randi Educational Foundation, which he established in 1996, claims that it will pay $1 million to any psychic who comes forward and produces indisputable proof of his or her abilities. Many have been challenged so far, but at the time of this writing, no one has yet stepped up to the plate.

Entertainers Penn Jilliette and Teller have been performing their comedic magic act for more then twenty-five years. The well-respected duo has lectured extensively and even served in the prestigious capacity of "visiting scholars" at the Massachusetts Institute of Technology. And part of their shtick, as you may well have guessed, is exposing psychic fraud. In 2003, Penn and Teller hit the airwaves with their much-acclaimed *Penn and Teller: Bullshit*. In the half-hour Showtime program, they trick and expose, antagonize and exploit, and try and trip up those they believe to be frauds.

One of the main roles of today's psychic is that of "entertainer." Today's mediums travel the world, providing engaging forums for spirit communication, like John Edward (see page 91), John Holland (see page 143), and James van Praagh (see page 211). Others, well before this generation, have gained notoriety by predicting future events, sometimes even hundreds of years past their own lifetimes, like Nostradamus (see page 183) and Mother Shipton (see page 199). Psychics have been enlisted to help solve crimes, like Dorothy Allison (see page 7), Peter Hurkos (see page 153), and Elizabeth Joyce (see page 157); and, in the most extreme cases, have even established new schools of thought, like Madame Blavatsky (see page 35) and Aleister Crowley (see page 69).

In the words of the immortal Robert LeRoy Ripley: Believe it or not. This is a collection of profiles of the life and times of the world's most famous and infamous psychics. No supposition is made that their work has been true or false, and, after reading countless tracts and watching endless series and documentaries, I've been through what most of us go through when we filter through this kind of information and try to decide if we believe or don't, and why or why not. I've been wracked with insomnia over the pending end of the world and the rise of Atlantis out of the sea; I've been plagued with fear that the writing I've been doing is somehow "automatic"—and what the plagiaristic ramifications of that might be in the spiritual domain. I've been riddled with guilt that deceased relatives may have been privy to my actions when I was being naughty. And then I've given myself a good swift kick reminding myself that there was one thing I knew was, without any doubt, real: my deadline.

The main conclusion to be drawn is that while the common perception is that those who believe are taking the "easy way out," one mustn't overlook the fact that belief is subjective at best, and disbelief, at times, much easier to understand and cope with. For example, if you decide not to believe that a great shift of the earth on its axis will upset the balance of life as we know it in 2012, as many in this book claim, you'll be more inclined to go on with the normal machinations of your life; if you believe, however, you certainly have a lot to accomplish in the next several years.

Whatever you believe, try not to scoff, nor let yourself get too sucked in by these tales. Instead, permit yourself to be entertained by the rich life stories of people who forged a different path, who moved from rags to riches—and sometimes on to ridicule.

From whatever side of the fence you are typically inclined to judge the type of information you are about to absorb, approach the facts and fabrications with an open mind. Make a willing suspension of disbelief; take an unheard-of-in-our-time leap of faith. Above all, think of this not as an attack or a defense, but merely as a survey of the most significant "extrasensory preceptors" of all time, of those who have made names for themselves by succeeding or sometimes shamefully failing to dazzle and delight with their "gift," and, even if just for an isolated moment, who have murked the all-too-tenuous line between belief and bullshit; between miracle and myth.

A

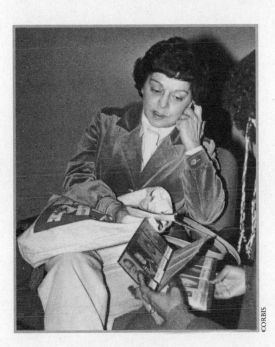

CORBIS

Dorothy Allison
Psychic Sleuth
(1925–1999)

If it's something of mine and I lose it, I can't find it.
—Dorothy Allison

If a statement like this one fell from the mouth of your own great grandmother, you probably would just accept it. But coming from Dorothy Allison, it can induce a chuckle if you know anything at all about her work.

Dorothy Allison was a woman, who, more so in her advanced years than ever before, made a name for herself as someone who could "find" things—okay, people, living or dead—by relying on "visions." For more than thirty years, she used her telepathic clues to aid police investigations. Sometimes she helped, sometimes she hindered, but she was nothing if not earnest and typically beloved by the law enforcement officers and agents whom she assisted. She never promised to have all the answers. "I give them what I got," she said, describing her involvement in the process, "and they do what they want with it."

For most of her life, Allison lived in the quiet suburb of Nutley, New Jersey. Although she was the mother of three, grandmother of seven, and great grandmother of four, don't think she spent the majority of time in her kitchen baking cookies and preparing Sunday dinners. Sure, she did that, too, but her kitchen served another purpose. At her kitchen table was where she would "work"—not on cakes and casseroles, but on crimes. Allison could often be found sitting there, poring through photographs of strangers, a pensive stare fixed on her face. The pictures were generally those of the missing and/or presumed dead, and as she perused the photos, clues would come to her.

Allison reported being involved in some 5,000 investigations. Sometimes, the police came to her with a missing persons story they couldn't seem to close, but many times, a tidbit, a flash would spark.

Was she a godsend or a nuisance? That all depends on whether or not you believed her. Robert DeLitta, chief of the Nutley Police Department and someone who had worked most closely with her, was fond of Allison. "The information she provided was very, very accurate—right on the money," he has said.

However, there were others who did not—and still don't—buy into her sleuthing skills, not so much cops who actually worked with her, but skeptics. Mostly, they believe that Allison got her information through a process called "retrofitting," that she had been able to find certain facts, possibly buried in the newspaper, and she built her "predictions" by connecting together these snippets of what she already knew. And then, of course, there's common sense. As Michael Shermer of *Skeptic* magazine scoffed of Allison's ability to detect where a body may have been disposed, "if you have a body, are you going to dump it in a crowded city?"

Allison didn't waste a lot of time fighting her detractors. She, too, was always suspicious of extrasensory ability—of others, that is. "If you asked me if I believe in psychics," she said, "I'd say no— only very few."

Unlike other psychic sleuths, Allison never charged a penny for her contributions, except for expenses reimbursement, so, really, who was she hurting if she got something wrong? Some have complained that she wasted man-hours, but in the worst-case scenarios, if she'd been too convincing with a wrong prognosis, the real perpetrator might be getting away while the police chased her psychic windmills.

The first case for which Allison was in the spotlight concerned the disappearance of a local boy. Allison called the police and tipped them off that the boy was, unfortunately, dead and that she had psychically seen his body in a drainpipe. Much work was done to recover the body from where Allison thought it was, but to no success. Eventually, the body was found, but floating in a pond—not in a drainpipe. Skeptics say she was wrong, she botched the investigation, and she cost the city thousands of dollars with the expense of drainpipe dismantling; however, it should be noted that she was right about at least one thing: the child had drowned when he could have fallen victim to any number of other horrors.

Most people accepted this much, and as her accuracy grew, she began to be more and more trusted, and soon found herself involved in some pretty high-profile cases.

In 1974, she entered the investigation for the kidnapping of Patty Hearst, who had been abducted in February of that year. While Allison could not tell the Hearst family exactly where the Symbionese Liberation Army (SLA) had been hiding Patty, she was able to tip them off that the kidnappers were going to brainwash Patty into robbing a bank. By May of that year, Patty was fully involved with the SLA, calling herself "Tania" and helping the group in its efforts, including robbing a bank.

Allison also got involved in the Son of Sam slayings. She couldn't definitively pin down the true identity of the killer, but she did surmise that he would be found through some connection to a parking ticket. Shortly after Allison made her prediction, police found David Berkowitz, a.k.a. Son of Sam, through a parking ticket.

As her visions intensified, so did her caseload. Some of the investigations she found herself involved in were so gruesome, however, that she nearly wanted to quit. "At one point I was so upset by the tragedies I was seeing that I wasn't sleeping. I wanted to give the whole thing up," she told *Good Housekeeping*. "Then a woman called and begged me to help find her daughter. How could I refuse? I figured God must want me to do this." So she trudged on.

Anyone at all familiar with the murders that occurred in Scarborough, a suburb of Toronto, Canada, in the late 1980s and early 1990s would especially understand Allison's not wanting to see all the vile things one human being can be capable of doing to another, especially considering all the abominable things Paul Bernardo and Karla Homolka did to their victims. But the visions continued, so in March 1991, Allison called Scarborough police to help.

Allison learned that one of the first victims, Melanie Hall, had been reported missing, so she asked for information such as date of birth and other essentials about the girl to do her chart. The outlook was grim: Allison saw a dismembered body, its parts encased in an array of cement blocks, one with a leg "popping out."

Months later, another girl, Lisa Mahaffy, disappeared, and Allison predicted the same fate had befallen the girl. Within a couple of weeks, both bodies turned up. And, much to the disgust of Allison and, well, amazement of believers, the bodies were found chopped into pieces and encased in cement. And Hall's leg jutted out of its cement coffin.

Allison was contacted again when another girl disappeared; she told Scarborough police that another body was going to turn up, though this time, it would not be dismemberment but strangulation. Two weeks later the body of Kristen French was found. Cause of death: strangulation.

Allison's last high-profile case was the JonBenet Ramsey murder. Allison was adamant that the parents did not do it. She even gave the Boulder, Colorado, police the real killer's description, and they came up with a composite sketch. To date, the true identity of the killer remains a mystery and one that Allison will not be able to help solve. About a year after she helped make the sketch, in December 1999, the seventy-four-year-old psychic sleuth died of heart failure.

AP WORLDWIDE

Rosemary Altea
Medium
(c. 1940s–)

The wonder and the joy and the information that comes with acknowledging your spiritual self is so transforming that many people are afraid that it is going to transform them to the point where they

> *won't know their lives anymore. . . . The only thing*
> *that comes from discovering who you are and learning*
> *to get to know your spiritual self, whatever changes*
> *take place, will only enhance their lives.*
>
> —A message from Rosemary Altea,
> on her Web site

When Rosemary Altea published her first book, *The Eagle and the Rose*, in 1995, it shot to the top of the *New York Times* best-seller list. It was not a book she wrote on her own, but in conjunction with her spirit guide, Grey Eagle, a long-deceased Apache Native American who speaks to her from the Other Side. It would seem that in the modern, scientifically sophisticated and brutally cynical world, a book about living with spiritual gifts, with one of the authors writing from the hereafter, may cause speculation and scorn—but it's clearly the opposite. In fact, people can't get enough of the British psychic and her Apache sidekick, as evidenced by the best-selling status of all their collaborations.

It's only been since the mid-1970s that Rosemary has openly shared her experiences in the other realm, but she always knew there was something different about her.

Born in the 1940s in Leicester, England, Rosemary had a highly escapable, abusive in all kinds of ways, childhood. Her father, William Edwards, was a stern military man with the Royal Engineers. He had very little patience for his little girl and, purportedly, physically abused her—and often. What her mother lacked in physical abusiveness, she more than made up for in mental and emotional damage. Lillian Edwards was not a loving, accepting, nurturing mommy type, but rather a brass ice queen with little tolerance for anything, especially her young daughter.

Psychic abilities may have run in Rosemary's family, but neither her father nor her mother was open to the possibility. This was fully evidenced when her parents called the "men in the white coats" to dramatically drag away Rosemary's grandmother, Eliza, when Rosemary was still a little girl. Apparently, Eliza had been having "visions," and Rosemary's ever close-minded parents assumed this was some kind of old-age-related dementia.

Rosemary knew her grandmother's visions couldn't have anything to do with her grandmother's age because ever since she could remember, Rosemary had been having visions herself. "Ever since I was a child, I have been visited by those in the spirit world, seen faces in the night, and heard whispering voices," she reports on her Web site. When she admitted as much to her mother in an effort to rescue her grandmother from the lunatic asylum, Chilly Lillian told her she should keep such nonsense to herself. Terrified the same fate would befall her, Rosemary did just that, all the while growing up and spending a fair portion of her adult life believing she was insane.

In 1965, Rosemary married a clothing company manufacturer and once and for all moved far away from Leicester and her miserable life. But the one thing she could not get away from were the visions.

In the mid-1970s, when Rosemary was about thirty-four or thirty-five, her openly philandering husband abandoned her and her ten-year-old daughter, Samantha. While she was devastated at the time, the events of the next few years would prove it was the best thing that could have happened to her.

On top of her emotional devastation, Rosemary was also quite destitute. Desperately needing money, she got a job as a barmaid to pay the bills. As she was still having her visions, it occurred to her that maybe now was the time to see if she could try using her talent in a way that could help support herself and her daughter. So she took the first step and joined a small spiritualist group, whose members eventually helped build and nurture her gifts.

At that time, she was also formally introduced to her spirit guide, who had always been with her, but whom now she was finally ready to acknowledge and *see*. "Grey Eagle is tall, very broadset, and handsome," she has said. "He has incredible almond-shaped eyes. His presence exudes real power and strength and at the same time, an incredible gentleness."

The more communication she had with Grey Eagle, the more

she understood about her talents and her mission. "With the help of my spirit guide," she reports on her Web site, "I have learned to communicate with the dead, discovered the power, helped rescue lost souls, and more." Since she first accepted him into her life, she and Grey Eagle have been inseparable.

By 1982, Rosemary was ready to begin her own practice. She had now fully accepted her powers and knew what she was meant to do with them. Not only was she *not* insane, but she could use her talents to help others. She was finally free of the insecurities that came out of her upbringing. "It was like coming out of the darkest dungeon and stepping out into the sun," she told *People Weekly*.

Every medium has a way to describe how he or she communicates with the spirit realm and how he or she is able to bring through messages from people whose languages he or she doesn't even speak. Rosemary explains it this way: "I think words are only sounds we make with the energy that we have. I think the power of our thoughts is way more powerful and way more positive. We have to have a thought before we can form a word." In other words, Rosemary reads thoughts and energy before they become words and language.

Inspired by her work and looking forward to sharing it with as many people as she could, Rosemary published *The Eagle and the Rose*. In it, she chronicles her life story—an inspiring account of surviving a less-than-loving childhood and a rocky, faithless marriage, and of discovering her mission. With Grey Eagle's help, Rosemary talks about what it took to come to terms with and then to harness her powers, and what it's like to be able to heal, to astral travel, and to perform soul rescues. According to Altea and Grey Eagle, those who die in childhood grow up, and deceased pets are happy and looking forward to being reunited with their owners, whom they don't forget. Spouses who have passed before look after, protect, and guide their widowed others. She also details ten of her own specific experiences with the afterlife.

Her second book, *Proud Spirit* (1997), shares more stories and insights that those from the spirit realm have shared with her. In *You Own the Power* (2000), Rosemary and Grey Eagle claim that anyone has the power to communicate with loved ones in the spirit realm; she presents simple, proven exercises that purport to help others wake up the power within, nurture it, and use it to help others. And in *Give the Gift of Healing* (1997), she instructs how anyone can spiritually heal him- or herself, and then broaden that talent to healing others.

Craving a larger venue through which to help people harness their own healing abilities, Rosemary and Grey Eagle founded the Rosemary Altea Association of Healers (RAAH), a charitable organization in England in 1981. The mission of this association is essentially to promote healing—as an art and a science—and encourage people to develop as healers. By 1986, RAAH's first center had opened in northern England. There are several of these centers operating today, though none as of yet have been opened in the United States.

These days, Rosemary, who now divides her time between living in Vermont and England, is much too busy to see people privately anymore. However, she continues to help others through her gift—on a grander scale. In addition to her prolific publishing efforts, she does as much media as she has time for. She has been featured on *The Oprah Winfrey Show*, *Larry King Live*, and other top television shows. She's been interviewed extensively by many and diverse publications including *Vanity Fair*, *Elle*, *Entertainment Weekly*, *People Weekly*, and the *New York Times*.

Naturally, Rosemary has detractors. On an episode of *Bullshit*, Penn and Teller set up the medium by planting one of their people as a "sitter" into one of her gatherings. They proclaimed with the footage they ran that they had exposed Rosemary "cold reading"—meaning, she was throwing out questions and scooping up the right answers based on the sitter's reactions to what she was asking.

Rosemary doesn't let skeptics get in the way of her mission. She doesn't explain herself, nor does she feel she needs to. She simply continues with her work, knowing that not everyone is going to accept what she does, but confident and satisfied in the fact that she's fulfilling her destiny and helping to move along the destinies of so many others.

George Anderson
Medium
(1952–)

I am only the instrument.
—George Anderson

George Anderson has known he was a medium since his childhood; however, it's only been since the mid-1970s that he's actually been openly using his gift. Anderson, it must be noted, is *strictly* a medium. He makes no predictions and cannot read minds; he simply relays messages from the dead. How does he know he's about to be contacted by the spirits? "I feel a whirring in my head, very much like a generator starting up," he told *People Weekly* in 1999. "And while I am discerning I am part of the exhilarating electromagnetic forces that souls use to transmit their messages."

According to his Web site, Anderson's visions started coming to him after he got the chicken pox when he was about six years old. Highly religious his entire life, he found the discovery of his psychic gifts jarring at first. There was no room for paranormal ability in his faith system and he was terrified of the ramifications. And if it scared him, it especially worried those around him. In fact, when he was sixteen years old, he was almost committed to a mental hospital because of it.

Having endured and survived his rocky and troubled "hallucination-riddled" adolescence, he finally began tuning into the spiritual realm in his twenties. Those who had previously doubted his sanity soon began to see that he was "for real," with his reported accuracy rating of 85 percent. Around about 1975, he fully accepted his destiny and started helping others.

He's been unstoppable ever since.

In 1982, Anderson became the first medium to have his own cable TV program, *Psychic Channels*. In 1987, syndicated radio talk-show host Joel Martin, who had interviewed Anderson profusely over a twelve-year period, collected some of Anderson's recorded visions and messages of "hope, truth, peace, and, above all, love," and compiled them into book form. The result, *We Don't Die: George Anderson's Conversations with the Other Side*, became an international best seller. In the book, among other revelations, Anderson explains that the reason he is not 100 percent accurate is due to human error, both his own and from those he is helping. It is also explained that much of the information he receives is not conveyed through words, but mostly through images and symbols, thus making the messages more open to misinterpretation.

Other books followed. In *Our Children Forever: George Anderson's Message from Children from the Other Side* (1996), Anderson talks about his experiences communicating with children who have died, and delivers to parents their messages of love and hope. In 1999, he wrote and published *Lessons from the Light: Extraordinary Messages of Comfort and Hope from the Other Side*. In this, he describes the afterworld in painstaking detail, tells readers what they can expect after they die, and gives advice on how, in the living world, they can work to ensure that their experience in the hereafter is satisfying and rewarding.

His most recent book, *Walking in the Garden of Souls: George Anderson's Advice from the Hereafter for Living in the Here and Now* (2001), Anderson expands on his description of the afterlife, conveying that it is also our "before life," telling readers, "It is a place we will see again only after our lifetime of struggle, hardship and hurt has earned us the reward of true and final peace."

In 1991, Anderson went under scrutiny and was subject to countless university challenges to prove what he claimed: namely, that he could communicate with the spirit world. Having aced the tests, by 1993 he began to make regular appearances on nationally syndicated talk shows and was featured in magazines and newspapers. So internationally impactful was he in the early 1990s, in fact, that he has been the only medium invited to Holland by the Anne Frank family. In 1995, they summoned him to communicate with their famed deceased relative.

Anderson loves what he does, and loves most that in communicating with the dead, he can bring joy and relief to the living. "I get to see the faces of the bereaved light up like the first blush of true love, and love fills a broken heart, if only for a while," he says.

"The love" is what Anderson stands on as his main reason for pursuing his vocation. Always one who has wanted to "give something back," Anderson began the Foundation for Hope, a nonprofit extension of his other organization, George Anderson Grief Support Systems, in 1997. Through these organizations, he tries to touch as many people as he can with his message and help them effectively deal with grief.

In 2001, Anderson was back on television again with his new primetime show, *Contact: Talking to the Dead*. The most controversial spirit he brought through this venue was that of the recently murdered Bonny Lee Bakley, wife of actor Robert Blake, when members of her family were guests of the show. As of 2004, however, according to his management, George Anderson no longer does any media, devoting himself wholly to his organizations.

If there's one phrase that sums up George Anderson's mission, it's this: All you need is love. The ever-amiable Anderson constantly encourages people to love one another and assures them that what "souls in the hereafter constantly tell is that love is what survives our physical bodies."

Apollonius of Tyana

Prophet, Healer

(exact dates unknown, but he lived well into his eighties—
first century–second century C.E.)

*I have seen men who inhabit the earth, yet do not live
on it, who are protected on all sides though they have
no means of defense, and who nevertheless possess
only what all men possess.*

—Apollonius of Tyana

Throughout time, Apollonius of Tyana has been compared to Jesus of Nazareth, and for many logical reasons. Both lived around the same time and wandered extensively, spreading good will, sprinkling miracles about, healing the sick, and bringing the dead back to life. Both had the charm and charisma to carry a crowd of followers, devoted even after their leader had departed this world. And neither left a corpse.

Of course, there are plenty of differences as well. Unlike Jesus, Apollonius grew up wealthy with every advantage imaginable. And his popularity remained fairly consistent; while there were those who scorned him, this was a small group. He did not generate anywhere near the level of controversy that Jesus did, and he was not executed for spreading his message; Apollonius lived to a rather ripe old age.

Apollonius came into the world under very extraordinary circumstances—almost as extraordinary as those in which he left it. As the legend goes, his very pregnant mother was wandering around a meadow one day, contemplating her pending motherhood. Feeling tired, she decided to lay down for a few moments and take a rest. Just then, a flock of wild swans descended on the meadow, squawking, crying, and beating their wings; almost as soon as they had come, however, they were gone, and within moments, Apollonius was born.

In the modern world, Apollonius's youth would be described as "charmed," filled with luxury beyond the limits of the wildest imaginations. In fact, his father was one of the richest men in the province. Apollonius was said to be extremely good looking, highly intelligent, personable, and, of course, charming. And let's not forget that he was ridiculously rich.

However privileged he was, even when he was very young, he did not plan to spend his life resting on his platinum, gold, and gem-encrusted laurels; rather, he made it a point from a very early age to strive to be as exceptional as he could possibly be, to leave his mark and make a difference in others' lives. Roughly 2,000 years later, it's pretty fair to say that he succeeded.

Apollonius was aware of his psychic abilities from the time he was a small child. He took the gift very seriously, weighing it against the other gifts life had so generously thrown at his feet—namely wealth, women, and wine. He chose wisdom, his psychic wisdom, and all accounts agree that he lived a life both virtuous and vino-free, sober and chaste, and focused fully on how he could use his talents to help others.

So when Apollonius was old enough, he left his father's house and all of its earthly trappings. He moved to Aegae, where there was a temple to Asclepius. This famed temple housed priests, philosophers, and doctors and drew visitors from as far away as Egypt. It was at this temple that Apollonius cut his teeth as a healer. Soon, he took on a kind of bohemian lifestyle, refraining from eating meat, wearing simple, basic clothing, and fast becoming the healer people traveled to see. While at the temple, he imposed a four-year vow of silence on himself.

And then it was time to move on again.

During his period of silence, Apollonius did a lot of meditating, looking for an answer to the age-old question of what it was he was meant to do with his life and how he was supposed to get to that point. It eventually came to him that he needed to seek out the spiritual wisdom of the mystics, so he decided to head to India. Apollonius was determined to bring the wisdom he would glean back to use toward the greater good of his people. He also decided that he would travel alone.

On his journey, he took a break to visit the temple of Dahnanean Apollo. There, he met a disheveled, scattered, absentminded priest, who offered him food and lodging. Apollonius enjoyed the old guy, so he decided to take him up on his offer to stay the night. And it was a good thing he did.

The meeting turned out not to be "chance," but fate. The priest had in his possession a temple treasure of thin sheets of copper with figures and diagrams etched on them. He had never been able to make heads or tails of the copper pieces, but for some reason, he thought his young guest would know what they were for. He was right. Apollonius knew exactly what the message was. On the pieces was a map left by Pythagoras, a former famed journeyer to mystic wisdom. The map not only showed the location of the exact destination to which he needed to travel in India, it also let him know

21

who he was to see once he got there. The priest was awed; another lifetime admirer of the young clairvoyant was made.

On the next leg of his journey, Apollonius stopped at Mespila. There he met Damis, who decided he would tag along with the lone wanderer. Damis had no psychic powers of his own and he soon realized who the more popular traveler of the two of them was going to be. So Damis jovially accepted his role as "sidekick," especially if it meant he would be able to spend more time with Apollonius, who greatly intrigued him.

When they arrived in India, Apollonius stopped himself and his companion in their tracks. There they stood waiting for their teachers, who materialized in minutes.

Apollonius and Damis sat with the wise ones for months, soaking in every last drop of ancient wisdom they could absorb. Cutting through the esoterica, the gist of those meetings was this: Apollonius was told he should wander the world, healing and performing miracles and helping as many people as he could. This, the mystics told him, is what had been divined by God, and so it must be.

Overjoyed that he finally had a mission in life, Apollonius thanked his teachers and left them with these parting words, "I came to you by land and you have opened me not only to the way of the sea but, through your wisdom, the way to heaven. All these things I will bring back to the Greeks, and . . . I shall continue to speak with you as though you were present." Throughout his life, he did just that.

The dutiful Apollonius went on to perform astounding feats. He exorcised many demons and made countless predictions.

In trying to affect a cure for an ascetic who had lost his powers, he discovered that the man was in fact the reincarnated Palamedes, a poet and scholar whose name has been lost to history, as Homer did not include him in the Iliad.

Apollonius immediately headed to Troy and learned that Palamedes had lost his life as a result of a treasonous letter penned by Odysseus. As soon as he had ascertained this, he divined the location of where a statue of Palamedes had once stood and ordered an excavation of the site. Out of the earth, the statue was found and placed back on its rightful spot aboveground. The moment the statue was back in place, the ascetic got his powers back.

Apollonius brought a young girl back to life when her funeral procession passed him. He saved his friend and disciple, Mennipus of Corinth, from marrying "a vampire." During the wedding feast, he made all the food, drink, and people disappear, causing the bloodthirsty bride to break down and admit that the accusation was indeed true. He escaped indictment by Nero by willing the information on the tablet that lay out the grounds for his arrest to be erased.

Apollonius is also thought to have written several books, including one on astrology, though this has never been definitely proven.

Stranger than the circumstances of Apollonius's birth and nearly more remarkable then the things he did in his life was the way his life ended. According to popular belief, when it was his time to go, the octogenarian simply disappeared, body and all, leaving in his wake a mystery that has survived 2,000 years.

B

Biblical Prophets

Elijah, Isaiah, Amos, Jonah, Ezekiel,
Jeremiah, Daniel the Prophet,
John the Baptist, St. John the Divine

This is the revelation given by God to Jesus Christ so
that he in turn could tell his servants about the things
which are now very soon to take place. The Lord sent
his angel to make these events known to his servant

> *John, and John has written down everything he saw,*
> *and swears it is the word of God guaranteed by Jesus*
> *Christ. Happy the man who reads this prophecy, and*
> *happy those who listen to him, if they hold fast to all*
> *that it says—because the Time is close.*
>
> —Revelations 1:1–3

Why have biblical prophets been included in a book on psychics? That's easy: It's because they are just that. Let's get back to the definition we're using for psychic: A person "who is born with or develops many gifts in the area of ESP, clairvoyance, communication with the spirit world, abilities to read the human aura and uses these special skills as a healer or reader." The prophets of the Bible are in touch with a realm that is not of the physical; they make predictions, provide advice as given to them from the spiritual world—in this case, God—and therefore, are undeniably "psychic."

Now, it would be impossible to include all the prophets of the Bible in this collection: there are literally hundreds of them, both prominent and obscure. Also, the most famous religious and not necessarily biblical prophets—namely Moses and Jesus as well as Mohammed—have also not been included. That said, it is interesting to note that many of the biblical prophets, John the Baptist especially, figure prominently in the teachings of other religions, including Islam.

The following are the stories of some of the most memorable biblical prophets.

Elijah

Elijah is one of the most famed prophets of the Old Testament, and the one to whom credit is most given in predicting the life and work of Moses and the first coming of Jesus.

Elijah was kind of shaggy, dressing in a camel skin he tied at the waist with a belt, and about as blunt as a person could be. He made no time for fancy talk and ceremonious preaching productions: receive the message, deliver the message, and move on. His message from God was that it was time for the ancients to stop wasting their time worshipping their many gods. Elijah barked at them that there was only one God and that they were annoying Him with their idolatry.

Many psychics produce "miracles"; they make things happen that cannot be explained or be believed if not witnessed firsthand. One of the most significant miracles that Elijah is known for is more of a contest that he arranged between the prophets of Ba'al, the prophets of Asherah, and himself, the sole prophet of the one true God, Yahweh. The contest was to take place in front of the people of Israel on Mount Carmel. The call to the various gods was to prove whose god was the true "God" by igniting their altars with fire. The two other groups went about their animal sacrifice and rituals, to no avail; nothing happened to their altars. When Elijah went to work with his ritual, however, his altar burst into flames.

They doubted him, so he had to rebuild the altar again, this time using wet stones. Despite this, the altar was soon ablaze, and the miracle could not be denied.

Elijah made several predictions against the house of King Ahab, and each came true. He said that the king would be murdered and dogs would lick his blood. Lo and behold, Ahab was murdered, in Samaria, and it is reported that dogs, in fact, did lick his blood. Elijah also postulated that after Ahab's death, his kingdom would perish and that his progeny would never rule. Right again. The prophet also said that Ahab's queen, Jezebel, would be devoured by dogs by the wall of Jezreel, and this, too came to pass.

Elijah's death is a miracle in and of itself as he never actually "died"; instead, when it was his time, he was reportedly "taken up in a whirlwind" sent from God.

Isaiah

It is believed that Isaiah had been a priest who preached not so much religious messages as political ones—less about following the word of God and more about people's actions and how they were affected by the overall state of the known world. His first prophecy came to him in the year King Uzziah died (c. 742 B.C.E.).

Essentially, Isaiah prophesied about the inevitable demise of ancient cities in kingdoms such as Judah and Assyria. But it wasn't all doom and gloom. Isaiah predicted the rise of Kind David, a spiritual renewal in Jerusalem, and the redemption of Zion.

The most significant prophecy of Isaiah was a vision of a "suffering servant," which has been interpreted by Christians as Isaiah's foretelling of the coming of Jesus.

As an interesting side note, some of the original books of Isaiah are, in part, what make up the Dead Sea Scrolls.

Amos

Known widely as the "prophet of doom," Amos is believed to be the father of the prophet Isaiah (see page 28). He lived in the eighth century B.C.E., beginning his life in the southern kingdom of Judah, in Tekoa. Of all the Biblical prophets, Amos was the most humble about the "gift" he had been given. In the book of Amos, he speaks of his calling—or, rather, of the way he perceived it: "I was no prophet . . . but I was a herdsman and gatherer of sycamore fruit: and the Lord took me as I followed the flock, and said to me, Go, prophesy unto my people Israel."

So, with no other pretense about him but his status as an ordinary shepherd, Amos wandered to Israel to give the people God's message. Simply put, they were not behaving in the manner in which God wanted them to behave. While they were keeping up with worshipping God, they were doing it unconsciously, half-heartedly, and, as Amos reported, with hypocrisy.

The main concern of the times was that the wealthy of the time were exponentially wealthy and the poor, which made up the majority of the people, were way over on the other side of the spectrum. Jesus' later message, "It is easier for a camel to go through the eye of a needle than for a rich man to enter the kingdom of God" was never more true.

Amos's mission was to warn the people of Israel that God was ferociously angry about all of these things, and that he was planning to strike down with furious anger on the people. This would come to pass in the form of an invasion from the Assyrians. And there was a catch: There was nothing the people of Israel could do to prevent this from occurring as God had already made up his mind.

Amos did also say, however, that God would be merciful and eventually forgiving, and would help the people rebuild their lives and their community after the attack, which, as the tale unfolds, was the case.

Jonah

Often known as the "prodigal prophet," Jonah was not in the least excited about the special gift of heavenly visions, which had been bequeathed to him by God. He couldn't be bothered. Instead, he generally tried to ignore God when He spoke to Jonah, and if God did happen to catch Jonah's ear, Jonah essentially disobeyed every order God gave him.

Jonah's big task was to convince the people of his native Nineveh that their worshipping of false idols was wrong and that great harm would befall the city if the practice did not stop. Not wanting to be one who tells others what to do—especially in an arena as controversial as idol worship—Jonah decided to hightail out of Nineveh, even taking a ship so he could get as far away as he could.

During the voyage, the ship was caught in a ferocious storm. The polytheistic crew tried to figure out a way to appease their angry gods, and they came to the conclusion that a man must be sacrificed to the sea. All the men of the ship drew lots, and when Jonah drew the short lot three times, it was time for him to go over the side.

After plummeting into the icy waves, Jonah was promptly swallowed by a whale. Inside the belly of the enormous beast, he prayed to God to set him free and he would do the work God had intended for him. God finally relented, and Jonah was spit back into the now-calm sea.

Returning to Nineveh, Jonah set to his task, but the people would not believe. Finally, God threatened to destroy the city in support of Jonah's message, and the people of Nineveh at last gave up worshipping their false idols and turned to the true God.

Ezekiel

One of the most important and revered of the Biblical prophets, Ezekiel spread his message for more than twenty years. Born about 627 B.C.E. into a world that was still recovering from the devastation God inflicted in the time of Amos, he was not exactly well-received by the people—at least not at first. His mission was to stop idolatry and remind the people about exactly whom they were supposed to be worshipping.

Ezekiel, like the prophets Jeremiah (see page 31) and Daniel (see page 31), lived in exile in Babylon. Babylon had conquered Assyria, and many from that region were taken from their home at the time.

An unusual character, Ezekiel, at God's prompting, would sometimes become a shut-in. An odd way for someone who's supposed to be out preaching messages, but God apparently wanted Ezekiel to set an example for the people. Also, allegedly, God imposed many unusual demands on the prophet, including eating unclean bread, shaving the hair off his head and his face, and tying himself up. Ezekiel was married early on, but his wife died shortly after his ministry began.

Ezekiel hadn't always known he was going to be a prophet. In fact, it wasn't until he was in his thirties that he began his life's work. As reported in the Book of Ezekiel, "the heavens opened, and I saw visions of God. On the fifth day of the month . . . the word of the Lord came to Ezekiel the priest, the son of Buzi, in the land of the Chaldeans by the river Chebar; and the hand of the Lord was upon him there."

Ezekiel prophesied about the destruction of Solomon's temple, the ruin of the homeland, and made several other doom-related revelations. Many of Ezekiel's prophecies appear again in St. John's Book of Revelation, including the New Jerusalem. Some have tied his prophecies to such ends as the Jewish Diaspora and the unrest in the Middle East.

How Ezekiel died is a mystery. Some say he lived to a ripe old age, others report that he was executed by the Babylonians.

Jeremiah

Jeremiah lived in the sixth century B.C.E. A contemporary of Daniel (see below) and Ezekiel (see page 30), Jeremiah's prophecies were also heavily laden with warnings of doom and disaster for the people of Israel. "Lo, I am bringing against you, O House of Israel, a nation from afar that declares the Lord. . . ," it reads in the Book of Jeremiah. "They will devour your harvest and food, they will devour your sons and daughters."

Like Ezekiel, Jeremiah's main mission was to scare people away from idolatry—and frighten them back into worshipping just the one Lord. He also was quite outspoken about his people, the people of Jerusalem, not fighting back when they were attacked by the Babylonians. He wasn't exactly happy with his job—he knew that many of the things he was saying made him seem traitorous and would probably be punished with the strictest of penalties: death.

Eventually jailed and executed, Jeremiah is noted especially for his prescience in the attack of Jerusalem by Babylon, and the ensuing exile of the people of Judah that would follow.

Daniel the Prophet

Theologians do not always recognize Daniel as a "prophet," but as more a "seer"; while he had many visions in his long lifetime of future events, his mission was not necessarily to "spread" the word of God.

Born into affluence in Jerusalem, Daniel lived in the fifth century B.C.E. When he was about sixteen years old, Jerusalem was invaded by the Babylonians, and Daniel was taken away to become one of the slaves of the king. Even though he would not follow some of the rules—the ones that went against the wishes of his God, like eating many of the rich meals he was expected to consume—he was in great favor with all three kings whom he served in his lifetime.

Daniel was known to be a very devout and holy man, and would pray to his God three times a day. He also had many visions and made predictions such as how the kingdoms of Greece, Persia, and Rome would come into existence and who their rulers would be.

One of the most salient predictions in the Book of Daniel is that of the coming of Jesus, which came to him in a vision:

> In my vision at night I looked, and there before me was one like a son of man, coming with the clouds of heaven. He approached the Ancient of Days and was led into his presence. He was given authority, glory, and sovereign power; all peoples, nations, and men of every language worshipped him. His dominion is an everlasting dominion that will not pass away, and his kingdom is one that will never be destroyed.

There are two legends that have immortalized Daniel. The first involves a prophecy dream of the king's that Daniel successfully divined and interpreted. His success in this led to Daniel interpreting dreams for kings for generations.

The second concerns the story of the lion's den. King Darius was tricked by people who wanted to see the much-favored Daniel out of the picture. They talked him into making a decree that anyone found praying to anyone but Darius in a thirty-day period would be thrown in the lion's den. When Daniel was caught praying, the decree could not be lifted and Darius hoped for Daniel that his "God" would protect him, which He did. Daniel avoided being devoured by the hungry lions, it is believed, as a miracle of God. When Daniel emerged unscathed, thousands were converted.

John the Baptist

Born six months before Jesus, John the Baptist is the last of the Old Testament prophets and one of the most remembered. It was John who not only prophesied that the son of God was on his way, but also, in his lifetime, saw his prophecy come true as he, and others, believed the son of God was none other than Jesus.

Not much is known about John's life before he turned thirty-two and began his famous mission, except that an angel foretold the birth of the son of Zacharias and Elizabeth. As the story goes, this rendered Zacharias speechless, literally, until John was born and circumcised.

Before John embarked on his mission, it is said that he escaped to the wilderness for forty days and forty nights, where he subsisted on a diet of locusts and wild honey. When he returned to civilization, he took on the appearance of Elijah: scraggly and dressed in the skin of a camel.

In an effort to prepare the world to receive the Lord when He came, John went around baptizing everyone. One day, Jesus came to be baptized and John, knowing who had come and feeling decidedly unworthy, respectfully refused, though Jesus insisted.

Months later, when he publicly denounced the king for carrying on with his own brother's wife, Herodias, John became a prisoner of King Herod. At a birthday celebration for the king, the daughter of Herodias, Herod's niece, Salome, performed the dance of the seven veils, which was so compelling to Herod that he promised the young nymphet, who was probably about fourteen at the time, anything in the world she desired, up to half his kingdom. The evil Herodias told her daughter to request the head of John the Baptist on a silver platter. And so it was.

Months later, each participant in the murder of John the Baptist was appropriately punished: Salome fell into a frozen pond, up to the neck, and while she "danced" underwater to set herself free, her head was severed from her neck. Herod's kingdom was invaded and taken over, and both he and Herodias were executed.

St. John the Divine

Not much is known about the life of St. John the Divine, who wrote Revelations in around 70 C.E.; however, his visions of heaven and hell and his apocalyptic prophecies continue to fuel nightmarish end-of-the-world fears.

One day, John was minding his own business, thinking about God, when all of a sudden he heard the blare of a trumpet and a voice that said, "Write what you see in a book and send it to the seven churches." When he turned around, he saw what he described as "seven golden lampstands" within which was "like a son of Man. . . . He was dressed in a long robe and had a gold band around his chest . . . his eyes were like flames of fire."

Before long, the vision pulled John up within it, and he was in heaven, where angels revealed to him the secrets of the seven seals.

While he was in heaven, he was given a rundown of the end of the world; of Christ's Second Coming, Judgment Day. The gist was that Christ will come again and that there will be a great battle between Christ and Satan, which Christ will win. After the battle is won, believers will go to heaven; nonbelievers and Satan will be banished to hell for all eternity.

From John's time to the present time, from Nostradamus (see page 183) to William Branham (see page 41) to Edgar Cayce (see page 61) and beyond, other visionaries have tried to pinpoint exactly when Judgment Day will be. No one's quite nailed it yet.

Helena Pertrovna Blavatsky
(a.k.a. Madame Blavatsky)
Clairvoyant
(1831–1891)

Helena Petrovna Blavatsky . . . is surely among the most original and perceptive minds of her time. . . . Buried in . . . two of her major books . . . there lies, in rudimentary form, the first philosophy of psychic and

> *spiritual evolution to appear in the modern West. . . .*
> *Madame Blavatsky may be credited for setting the*
> *style for modern occult literature.*
>
> —Theodore Roszak, *The Unfinished Animal:*
> *The Aquarian Frontier and the Evolution*
> *of Consciousness* (1975)

For many, the mere mention of the name "Madame Blavatsky" might immediately conjure up an image of a rotund, older woman with a meaty, weathered, jowly face fronting a babushka-wrapped head, with eyes that shift and squint as they peer into a crystal ball, as fortunes are doled out in a thick, nearly indescribable, Eastern European accent.

This isn't an incorrect picture of the woman who is widely known as the "mother of the modern spiritualist movement"; it's simply incomplete. For, on top of setting the stereotype for the carnival fortune-tellers everywhere, in her life Helena was many things: a traveler and vagabond, a wife and mother, a devotee of Eastern philosophies and teachings, an author, the founder of an innovative religious movement, and, yes, a psychic.

H.P. Blavatsky—as she is commonly known in her writings—was born on August 12, 1831, in southern Russia into a fairly remarkable family. Her father, Colonel Peter von Hahn, was a prominent figure in the Russian army. Her mother, Helena Andreyevna, nee Fadeyev, was a well-regarded novelist, known as the "George Sand of Russia," who wrote books about the plight of Russian women. She, the daughter of Privy Councillor Audrey de Fadeyev and Princess Helena Pavlovna Dolgorukov, was of noble descent. H.P.'s grandmother was also a writer, as well as a widely respected botanist.

Even as a child, Helena began showing signs of being somewhat different. A sensitive girl, she was highly neurotic and prone to convulsions and sleepwalking. But she was also in touch with nature and a talented musician and artist, which sometimes goes along with the territory. Additionally, she was in tune to realms not perceived by the five senses, which is something she would call on again and again in her life—for better or for worse.

One of the first instances of paranormal "weirdness" Helena recounts in her writings happened when she was just four years old. Russia, at the time, was ripe with superstitions, and Helena fit right in. In the countryside, it was believed that spirit nymphs called "russalkas" lived along the banks of rivers. One day, when she was being bullied by a much older boy, Helena put a curse on the boy that the russalkas would tickle him to death. Eerily, his body turned up on the banks of a nearby river a couple of weeks later.

Tragedy again struck with the death of her mother when Helena was only about twelve years old; but even though the woman did not live to see how the events of the coming years would unfold, she was sure of one thing about her daughter, as she divulged from her deathbed, "her life will not be that of other women, and she will have much to suffer." In the coming fifty years, the elder Helena's prophecy would be proven again and again.

After her mother's death, Helena was raised by her grandparents in an environment that, for Helena's free spirit, was likely somewhat suffocating. Helena had always been restless and rebellious toward authority, and she put that restlessness into effect when she escaped the confines of her grandparents' home by pretending to "settle into a normal life." In 1848, the seventeen-year-old Helena married the roughly forty-year-old General Nikifor Blavatsky.

The marriage was never consummated, and it wasn't long before Helena's free spirit took over again. Extricated from her marriage after barely a year into it, Helena chose not to belong to any one person, but to belong to the world. Over the course of the next few years, she lived like a vagabond, traveling throughout Europe, Turkey, Egypt, and the United States. Although she went everywhere, there was one place she most dreamed of visiting, and which she was only permitted to enter on her third try: Tibet.

Finally reaching her destination—and destiny—in the mid-1850s in Tibet, Helena began studying under the Lama. Here, she witnessed a highly influential reincarnation ceremony, while she absorbed the Eastern tenets that would eventually lead to the Theosophy movement, for which she is most remembered and which will be covered in greater detail a little later.

Even by twenty-first century standards, the idea of a young woman traveling the world by herself, having all the adventures and experiences she wants to have, is noteworthy. In the nineteenth century, the same situation was nothing short of remarkable, and as such, Helena was often scorned and reviled for her behavior. But she continued unapologetically, at least at the time. Years later, she wrote, "For over 15 years I have fought my battle for the blessed truth." She later wrote in the publication *The Spiritual Scientist* (1874), "For the sake of spiritualism I have left my house; an easy life amongst a civilized society, and have become a wanderer upon the face of this earth."

By the 1860s, when Helena was in her thirties, she took a break from her travels and decided to return to her husband, if only temporarily. Records vary during the early part of the decade about her relationship with General Blavatsky; there are accounts of other lovers—some of whom may have lived with the Blavatskys—and her antics at the time. Most sources agree on two points: to make a living, Helena held séances in her home; and second, she gave birth to a boy in 1861 or 1862, though sources disagree on who the father was. Whatever the case, the boy, Yuri, was born with serious deformities and barely lived to see his fifth birthday.

The grief Helena experienced resulted in a full-fledged nervous breakdown; when she recovered, it was time to hit the road yet again. In 1868, she headed back to Tibet where she absorbed more information from her masters; the seeds of Theosophy that had been planted through the years began to sprout.

Theosophy, derived from the Greek words "theos," meaning God, and "sophia," meaning wisdom, in Madame Blavatsky's own words, is like the white ray of the spectrum, and every religion one of the seven prismatic colors. . . . [A]s the sun of truth rises higher and higher on the horizon of man's perception, and each colored ray gradually fades out until it is finally re-absorbed in its turn, humanity will at last be cursed no longer with artificial polarizations, but will find itself bathing in the pure colorless sunlight of eternal truth.

In other words, only when all religions merge as one can universal peace and pure truth be enjoyed.

The fundamental principles of Theosophy are:

1. To form a nucleus of the universal brotherhood of humanity, without distinction of race, creed, caste, or color
2. To encourage the study of comparative religion, philosophy, and science
3. To investigate unexplained laws of nature and the powers latent in humans.

In 1873, Helena headed to New York, where she made a living the way she always had: by holding séances. As fate would have it, it was during one of her séances, this one in Vermont, that she made one of the most important relationships of her life: In 1874, Madame Blavatsky met Colonel Henry Steel Olcott, a man with a keen interest in Spiritualism and a plan to help Blavatsky spread her message far and wide.

In September 1875, back in New York City, Blavatsky and Olcott, along with William Quan Judge, began the Theosophical Society. Now with firm grounding, at the age of nearly forty-five, Helena began her writing career with her seminal work *Isis Unveiled* (1877). Many more volumes and several periodicals, all to advance the movement, followed.

In 1878, Helena was the first Russian to become an American citizen, though she opted to live in Bombay instead, where she launched more magazines. However, she suffered a particularly vicious attack by two of her former assistants, Emma and Alexis

Columb, which was followed up by a libel suit that Helena lost and that resulted in her leaving India in 1885, never to return. Helena died in 1891 in London, where a flu epidemic claimed her mortality—though her immortality persists.

When she was alive, the charismatic, colorful, and uncanny Blavatsky was attacked by skeptics, but she also did her share of attacking, generally in her books. In *Isis Unveiled*, she wrote: "The mercenaries and parasites of the press, who prostitute its more than royal power, will find it easy to mock at things too wonderful for them to understand; for to them the price of a paragraph is more than the value of sincerity."

One of the more hilarious attacks Helena made was the form of a stuffed baboon she displayed in her New York apartment. It wore a tweed jacket and carried a copy of *The Origin of Species* under its arm. This baboon was a visual attack on Charles Darwin, whose theories of evolution were completely out of whack with the teachings of Blavatsky's masters and also conflicted with the tenets of Theosophy.

Whether or not her life, as skeptics want folks to believe, was writhe with "scandals, shadows of lovers dead and gone, bigamous marriages, an illegitimate son, fraud and trickery *de luxe*" (as Gertrude Marvin Williams proclaimed in her famed 1946 attack, *Priestess of the Occult*), one thing is for certain: Theosophy today continues to thrive, and as more Western people become more comfortable with the tenets of the East, perhaps Blavatsky will be better understood. Perhaps she'll be seen less as a sham and a boisterous con artist and more as a world traveler who drew on her experiences to try to unite people under one belief system, a system in which all religions could peacefully coexist.

LIBRARY OF CONGRESS

William Branham
Mystic, Prophet
(1909–1965)

You got trouble in your side, setting [sic] right there,
that second person setting [sic] in from the end, there.
Don't you lady? You was healed just then of it. Stand
up, and just say—just say "Praise the Lord," for your
healing. God bless you.

> —William Branham, "testifying" before
> an audience in Chicago

While it was probably more common fifty or so years ago,
today people can still be found packed together in large

auditoriums—even stadiums—to listen to the words of one of God's purported messengers as he belts, at the top of his lungs, his preachings of sin and salvation. And maybe, if the crowd is lucky, he might just lay his hands on the sick and infirm and use his God-given powers to cure and heal.

It's an image we can all call to mind, whether we got it from television or movies, or even from personal experience. It's the picture of religious zeal taken to the nth degree. It's what happens when God "speaks to men directly" and appoints them to be messengers of His word. Or at least that's what they—and their followers—think.

All of this had to start somewhere, and while prophets have walked the earth since the dawn of time, this brand of preacher really began to pop up after William Branham lived and preached. Despite Branham's one-on-one demeanor of being humble and soft spoken, he is credited for sparking the charismatic and healing revival of 1947.

The pull the near-illiterate Branham had in his life can be appreciated in this 1961 quote from the *Full Gospel Businessmen's Fellowship International* (which, at the time, was known as *The Full Gospel Men's Voice*): "In Bible Days, there were men of God who were Prophets and Seers. But in all the Sacred Records, none of these had a greater ministry than that of William Branham. Branham has been used by God, in the name of Jesus, to raise the dead!"

Miracles and mysticism aside, Branham's personal life while he was growing up left much to be desired. Born into almost unbelievable poverty on April 6, 1909, the first of nine children of Charles, a raging alcoholic, and wife Ella, Branham's earliest days were spent in a remote log cabin in the hills of Kentucky. There was no such thing as "book learnin'" for the Branham children: the nearest school was miles away, and Charles and Ella, both painfully illiterate, were in no position to educate the children themselves, which was just as well for them, because they needed farm hands and there was no reason to go wasting any time on useless information like reading, writing, and 'rithmetic when there was keep to be earned.

The family later moved to Jeffersonville, Indiana, where there was a school the children could attend, but by that time it was too late for Branham to catch up. Throughout his life, he remained just barely literate.

Branham was reported to be a "nervous" child who was essentially ostracized by others for his "visions." His parents thought he was weird, but they had all those other kids to consider. Also, other children didn't want to be around him, which essentially created a void within him, a hole that he eventually patched up with devotion to God.

Branham was seven years old when God first "spoke" to him and said, "Don't ever drink, or smoke, or defile your body in any way. There will be work for you to do when you get older."

At the time, Branham didn't realize it was God speaking to him. In fact, it wasn't until he was fourteen that he finally figured it out. That year, he had an accident with a shotgun, which nearly killed him. (It's not known if he was playing with the gun, if someone else had aimed the gun at him, or even if his drunken father had set the gun off while he was cleaning it.) As William lay there, alone and dying, watching many visions of hell appear before him, he was inspired to call out to God. When he did, the visions disappeared and he was saved.

Branham may not have been an educated man, but he wasn't a stupid one, and if God had saved his life, by golly, he wanted to get in touch with Him so he could thank Him and also see how he could, in the simplest terms, pay Him back for the favor. The story goes that he paid back the debt not by going to church and praying, but by tacking a note to a tree. How he managed to scribble the right words out, however, considering that he could barely read or write, is a mystery.

In any case, God didn't get back to him right away, nor did he contact Branham directly—not this time. Eventually, Branham's call was answered by a townswoman he had met, Amelia Brumbach, who was part of the Missionary Baptist Church in Indiana. She invited Branham to join the congregation in 1931. From there, his mission was in motion. His obvious piety and devotion inspired the minister to encourage Branham to enter the ministry, and he was officially ordained in December 1932.

While Branham was performing a baptism in 1933, a light appeared over his head and he heard a voice. "As John the Baptist was sent to forerun the first coming of Christ," it said, "so are you sent to forerun his Second Coming!"

Also during that baptism, he was given, by God, the date of the Second Coming. Reportedly, he was told that "this age will end around 1977." Branham later reported that he based "this prediction on seven major continuous visions that came to me. . . . The Lord Jesus spoke to me and said that the coming of the Lord was drawing nigh, but before he came, seven major events would transpire."

Even later in life, Branham never read the scriptures. Essentially, he never needed to—not when he believed he had direct communication with God, who told him everything he needed to know in the form of visions.

Branham's admission of these visions was perceived, as can be imagined, as "blasphemy" by other ministers who were not graced by such visions. They considered it Satan's doing. As a result, Branham learned to keep many of his visions to himself and continued with his work. He was soon "punished" for his silence, however. In 1934, his first wife, Hope, and daughter, Sharon Rose, both died from tuberculosis.

The loss set him into a tailspin and he fled. Like so many prophets before him, Branham wandered through "the wilderness" for a spell, trying to figure out what it was God wanted from him.

In the wilderness, an angel appeared to him and told him the reason he was having all this bad luck was that he had ignored God's direct order to share His message with the world. When Branham explained to the angel that the reason he kept quiet was that others thought he was blasphemous, the angel assured him that he would be granted two more significant visions, and that all who were against him would soon follow him because of these visions.

Branham didn't need much more prompting than that. He returned to civilization and revamped his ministry. On command of the Almighty, he extended his missionary beyond his own parish and thus began a tour of the country.

He wasn't embraced by everyone, as can be imagined, and many times he wanted to give it all up. In May 1946, another angel appeared to him, the first of the aforementioned visions. The angel comforted Branham by explaining that his "peculiar gift and misunderstood life has been to indicate that you are to take a gift of Divine healing to the peoples of the world. If you will be sincere when you pray and get the people to believe you, nothing shall stand before your prayer, not even cancer."

Soon after, Branham learned he had the gift of healing and when it was made public, he earned a brand new crop of followers. Through his new power, he healed heart disease, cured cancer, and made cripples walk. He even caused the dead to rise, including a small boy in Helsinki, Finland, in 1950. The child had been killed when he was hit by a car and thrown from his bicycle. Branham happened to be passing the scene of the accident at the time. He stopped the car and approached the tiny, sheet-covered corpse. He placed his hand on the boy and soon the child began to breathe.

Through the magic of healing, Branham received nationwide attention, and soon the sheep were flocking to their new shepherd in droves. He remarried and began to spread his message around the world full-force, explaining his ministry was based on three "pulls": healing, prophesying, and revealing the word of God.

At his meetings Branham converted skeptics into believers, but he also turned off a fair share of them with some of the weird things he said. Wrapped up in the fervor of the love of God, Branham sometimes just got carried away. With the religious ecstasy of the massive crowds fueling him, he sometimes made very little sense, if any at all; "I preached with Moses and war—with Noah and warned the people of the oncoming judgment, to be a real Christian," he proclaimed. "I was with Moses at the burning bush. . . . I was with Moses up there in the wilderness. . . . I know what I'm talking about. I seen what happened, yes sir!"

On January 24, 1950, a photograph was taken of Branham in which what looked like a Pentecostal flame was burning over his head. Scientists and skeptics studied the image and no conclusion could be drawn as to what caused the "flame."

The second significant vision promised by the angel in the wilderness came to Branham on February 29, 1963, while he was on a hunting trip. Branham saw seven angels in a pyramid form in the sky above him. Soon, the pyramid sucked him up into it. There, the mysteries of the seven seals were revealed to him, which had only also been revealed to St. John the Divine (see page 34).

Branham's mission was halted shortly after the second vision, when he was only fifty-six years old. After a block of days of intense preaching, he was heading to his next meeting, when tragedy struck: On December 18, 1965, a drunk driver hit Branham's car in Amarillo, Texas. His second wife, Meda, and daughter were in the car, but they were not hurt. Branham, on the other hand, went into immediate shock and fell into a coma, from which he did not recover. With all the healing he had done in his life, he was not able to heal himself, and he died on Christmas Eve, December 24, 1965.

So broken up was Meda over his passing, she couldn't decide where to bury him, so, creepily enough, he was not put in the ground until April 11, 1966—more than four months after his death.

Dannion Brinkley

Clairvoyant

(1950–)

We are here on one mission and one mission only: to learn to love ourselves as we simultaneously learn to expand our love outwardly. The more love we give . . . the more the consciousness of the very universe grows.

—Dannion Brinkley

COURTESY OF DANNION BRINKLEY

Everyone, if lucky, gets a wake-up call to change the course of his or her life, to become a better person. For Dannion Brinkley, well, he had to be dead first.

Anyone who knew Brinkley in his early years would never have predicted that bad-ass, bad-boy Brinkley would become a comforter, helper, and humanitarian. He surely didn't see it. An epic transformation like that doesn't happen overnight, however, no matter the circumstances. To this day, Brinkley fights against what he perceives to be his true nature to live as the do-gooder he chose to become. In many ways, he's still "learning to be nice to people, which in all honesty, a lot of times is not one of my highest qualities." And yet, anyone who knows him today would never imagine the person he used to be.

Born in 1950, Brinkley was raised in near-poverty in rural South Carolina. Brinkley was in it only for himself from a very young age. He had a chronic bad attitude, which served him well in his role as school bully. After high school, he joined the U.S. Marines and brought his utter disregard for humanity with him: he became a government assassin—and even enjoyed his job.

After his stint in the military, he went into business for himself as a defense contractor. It was during an early-morning business telephone call when he was about twenty-five years old that lightning struck. Literally. An angry thunderstorm was raging outside, with bolts of lightning thrashing across the sky. One of those lightning bolts made its way through his phone line, striking Brinkley, who fell to the floor in a smoking heap.

Moments later, his girlfriend came in and found him lifeless. He knows this because he says he watched the action unfold from outside his body. He watched as an ambulance was summoned and he watched as paramedics descended on him.

And then all the images vanished and he was transported to a sea of amazingly bright white light. "From immense pain I found myself engulfed by peace and tranquility," he reports. "It was a feeling I had never known before and have not had since. It was like bathing in glorious calmness. I had no idea what had happened, but even in this moment of peacefulness I wanted to know where I was."

Before long, he was greeted by an angelic being, which led him through the Crystal City and into the Cathedral of Knowledge, where several other ethereal beings were waiting for him. There, he got his wake-up call—or at least his first wake-up call. The beings tossed thirteen "television sets" at him, each bearing its own vision on the screen. By the time they were through, Brinkley was given 117 glimpses of possible world events; by 2004, a significant number of them had come to pass, but we'll get back to that.

Visions of the future aside, the most remarkable thing that happened to Brinkley during his stay in the Crystal City was that he was let in on all kinds of secrets. He was forced to feel every bit of suffering he had ever inflicted on another human being. He experienced the last-minute confusion and the burning physical pain of those he had killed. And then he relived all the emptiness that had comprised his own life. "I now knew the simple secret to improving humanity," he says. "The amount of love and good feelings you have at the end of your life is equal to the love and good feelings you put out during your life. It was just that simple." The problem here, which you can guess if you've been following, was that he didn't have nearly enough of these good feelings and love, which meant eternity for him was going to be a bleak and barren void. Now knowing the truth, he yearned to change it all. But it was too late. He was dead. The die had been cast by his own hand; his eternal fate decided.

But then he got another chance.

Before he knew it, Brinkley was back in his own body, covered by a sheet and on his way to the morgue. He had been dead a remarkable twenty-eight minutes by the time he got back. The lightning had, literally, zapped all of his strength and he was too weak to alert hospital workers that he was alive. The only thing he could do was to blow up the sheet that covered his face. Finally, someone noticed, and he was whisked away to get special medical attention.

The recovery that followed was arduous. He was fully paralyzed for six days, and continued to be partially paralyzed for seven more months. Not having the capability to feed himself or get any kind of exercise, he ended up losing sixty-nine pounds. In the beginning of his recovery, no one had expected him to pull through. He was never given more than a week to live, every week, which he continued to defy. Essentially, his true nature helped him: He bullied death away.

It took two years before he fully recovered, but even after all of this, Brinkley admits he hadn't changed. He continued to be a jerk to others, and when he discovered his new gift, that he could now actually read minds, he abused it, using his new clairvoyant powers for gambling.

When he was in their world in 1975, the spirits had given him instructions to build centers for wellness. These centers were to be comprised of several rooms, including a therapy room, a massage clinic, a sensory deprivation chamber, a room with biofeedback machines, a room for readings, and a reflection chamber. He ignored everything he was told.

So the spirits called him back.

Amazingly, to date, Brinkley has had not two but *three* near-death experiences, and all to enforce messages he was given the first time and either forgot about or ignored. The first, which we already covered, was when he was struck by lightning at age 25. Note that the date of that one was September 17, 1975, at 7:05 A.M. The second occurred when he underwent open-heart surgery in 1989. The third occurred in the late 1990s—after he had written two books about what the spirits said. After suffering a brain aneurysm on an airplane, he had brain surgery, and slipped away for a while, weirdly enough, on September 17, 1997, at 7:05 P.M.

After his second near-death experience, Brinkley finally got his act together. He published a book about his first called *Saved by the Light* (1995). In it, he finally shared with the world what had transpired when he had died the first and second times and that he had learned from the spirits while he was dead. In 1996, he continued talking about these experiences in *At Peace in the Light*. Both books were best sellers.

In addition to spreading his "new attitude" message of goodness and light with the world, he has also divulged the prophecies shown him on the screens of the flying TVs. As of the present, nearly one hundred of the 117 have reportedly come to pass.

Way back in the 1970s, Brinkely predicted than an actor with the initials "R.R." would become president. That it was Ronald Reagan floored him: he was sure it would be Robert Redford. He also surmised that there would be great unrest in the Middle East, which was indeed a growing concern in the 1970s, so this wasn't that earth shattering. But he also said that Israel would become isolated from the rest of the world and that Saudi Arabia would buddy up with North Korea. Certainly, the events of even the recent past make the possibility of these seem much more likely than they would have back then.

Also predicted, and which has come to pass, was that in 1986, a nuclear explosion near a river in Russia would kill hundreds, and the disaster would be associated somehow with the word "wormwood." ("Chernobyl" is Russian for wormwood.) Also having to do with Russia, Brinkley saw a collapse of the Soviet Union due to economic problems. In 1989, the Soviet Republic dissolved. He also saw that in 1990 a desert war would be fought; Desert Storm commenced in January 1990.

But before getting too excited about all this, note that Brinkley generally does not make his prophecies public before they happen. "I don't like to tell too many predictions because if I do that I am committing them to reality. I'd rather talk about the good stuff." The spirits told Brinkley that humanity has the power to change the events of the future. Essentially, he feels that if the public knew about the events that might yet come to pass, which are not written in stone and thus could be changed if humanity pulled together, that they could become, well, self-fulfilling prophecies.

One of the prophecies that he hits on is one that many others chronicled in this book also postulate: "The earth is changing as the entire Universe is changing because between 2004 and 2014, more precisely between 2011 and 2012, we will experience the return of an energy system that existed here a long time ago," he says. "You can call it a spirituality uplifting consciousness, the Second Coming, or the birth of the Aquarian Age." Edgar Cayce (see page 61), Ruth Montgomery (see page 175), and others say that this is a shift of the earth on its axis, and that this shift will cause great physical as well as spiritual upheaval for humanity.

Today, in addition to his psychic work and altruistic concerns, Brinkley continues his work as a defense contractor. He also has a new passion: hospice care. Having passed over to the other side three times, he feels one of the contributions he can make to humanity is "necrophobic reduction"—that is lessening the fear of death. He started Compassion in Action to recruit hospice volunteers, and in 2001 was nominated for the National Hospice and Palliative Care Association's Heart of Hospice Award.

Brinkley continues to forge his mission. Says Brinkley, "People who give up fear of death give up stupidity and become sane. When you realize you don't die, which you don't, what you are giving up is a trap, an entrapment, that you have been in since conception. . . . The very moment that burden of fear is lifted from us, we begin to see life as a freedom, a wonderment, and a glorious time of change and evolvement."

COURTESY OF SYLVIA BROWNE

Sylvia Browne

Medium, Healer

(1936–)

*The world of dreams opens up ways for us to
release negative thoughts, to program positive ones,*

to reach loved ones who have passed, and even to
be precognitive.

—Sylvia Browne

Sylvia Browne is one of the most beloved psychics practicing today. Cheerful, as down-to-earth as she is in touch with the heavens, and as highly published and read as Danielle Steel, Browne is the "people's medium." On the flip side, however, are skeptics like magician James Randi, who distrusts Browne almost as much as John Edward (see page 91). For the skeptic community at large, she has of late become a target over Randi's famous test, which we'll get into a little later. Browne has essentially risen above Randi and other detractors, and her followers, for the most part, remain devout, unswayed, and convinced that she is about as far from being a fraud as the gruff, bearded Randi is a woman.

Born in 1936, in Kansas City, Missouri, Sylvia grew up with psychic ability all around her. Her grandmother, Ada, was an established psychic and healer in Kansas City, and she reportedly has many other psychic relations.

Sylvia was three years old when she discovered her talent. "When I was younger," she says, "I'd go into a crowd of strangers and automatically know who was getting divorced, who had a sick stomach, who had a brain tumor." As long as she can remember, she's been helping others with her talents, and she never received any special treatment—positive or negative—because of it. "As a kid, I wasn't treated any differently than anyone else," she has said. "[M]y head didn't turn around and I didn't spit pea soup."

In 1964, Sylvia started thinking about using her abilities more publicly, to help others, and decided to move to California, where she continues to live and practice today. At first, she only looked after the paranormal interests of neighbors and friends. Her professional psychic life finally began on May 8, 1973, with a small meeting in her home. The meeting was an incredible success, and word of her talent spread.

Her success was so viable, in fact, that the very next year, in order to accommodate her exponentially expanding practice, she started the Nirvana Foundation for Psychic Research. In 1986, the organization's name was changed to the Society of Novus Spiritus. Browne's Web site explains that the main purpose of the Society of Novus Spiritus is to train ministers to spread Browne's philosophies, which are that the soul survives death, that God is a real and loving presence, that there is a Divine plan to our lives, and that we are to establish a spiritual community that loves both male and female aspects of God, without the traditional trappings of sin and guilt associated with faith.

Throughout the years, Browne has used her deep trance channeling abilities and relied on her spirit guide, Francine, to help her get answers to the questions that plague believers. With Francine's help, all the information that makes up her books, lectures, appearances, and legacy comes through. Browne is not proprietary over her paranormal powers and believes others, if they get in touch with their spiritual selves, will be able to achieve the same level of communication she has mastered.

In 1989, Browne published her first book about her psychic work and mission. *Adventures of a Psychic* gives readers advice on how they might go about peeking at the other side. In 1999, she published *The Other Side and Back*, a number-one best seller that explains that the afterlife, or "heaven," is nothing more than the other side of this world, a place where souls take a break before being reincarnated into another life. She followed that up in 2000 with *Life on the Other Side: A Psychic's Tour of the Afterlife*, in which she gives readers an actual tour of what she's seen and experienced "over there." This time, she spent twelve weeks on the bestseller lists. In 2001, *Past Lives, Future Healing: A Psychic Reveals the Secrets to Good Health and Great Relationships*, also a best seller, teaches readers to let go of the baggage they may have accumulated in past lives and enjoy the life they are leading now.

Browne's latest book to tackle questions from the afterlife was published in 2003. In *Visits from the Afterlife: The Truth about*

Hauntings, Spirits, and Reunions with Lost Loved Ones, Sylvia talks about the connections she's made with the departed and takes the reader on a tour through various supernatural locations, like haunted houses and other venues where the now-dead once walked and breathed.

A media darling, Browne has shown her skills on many different television shows, from *Montel*, to *Larry King Live*, to *Sally Jesse Raphael*, to *Entertainment Tonight*, to *Unsolved Mysteries*. She's been profiled in *Cosmopolitan*, *People Weekly*, and many other magazines. She's also made several pay-per-view specials. Her hosts have proven to be as devoted as her followers. Montel Williams, on whose show Browne is a regular guest, says, "I've personally witnessed her bring closure to distraught families, help police chase cases, and open people's hearts to help them see the good within themselves."

As popular and perennially best selling as her books about the afterlife are, her books about dreams, a subject in which she is considered a foremost authority, are also very popular. In these books, she again makes the point that the abilities she possesses—channeling the dead, premonitions, and telepathy—can be actualized by anyone who dreams. What about people who say they don't dream? Browne explains, "All people dream, they just often go in too deep." For those who have trouble remembering dreams, she advises, "ask God before you go to sleep to help you remember your dreams, and keep a pen and paper by your bed to write them down as soon as you wake up."

Browne says a lot can come through in dreams, including experiences from past lives. She says, "Past life dreams usually come in a very distinct setting. Feeling of seeing yourself as an American Indian or in a Victorian setting . . . especially if it happens often, can indicate that you may have once lived in that time or place."

And now for the million-dollar question—and that's meant literally: Why is James Randi so hot under the collar at this God-loving, ever-helpful, seemingly well-meaning woman? On September 3, 2001, Randi challenged Browne with his famous test, the one he offers though his foundation, which will award $1 million to anyone who can scientifically substantiate psychic power. Randi feels he was lax with the requirements: He asked for thirty minutes of her time and said it could happen over the phone at any time of the day that would be best for her. He said he would produce a person chosen at random from ten final applicants and has at least offered to provide the name, gender, and age of the person selected.

He posed the challenge on *Larry King Live*; she accepted. And then she seemed to back out. She won't take Randi's test. Why?

Essentially, Browne doesn't feel like she has to prove herself to anyone anymore—least of all to Randi. "I've always fought for legitimacy and legality my whole life," she has said. "If you're the real thing, you don't need props. Look, I'm not against tarot cards and crystal balls," she continued, "but how'd you like to go to a doctor and he consults a pendulum? There's a false image genuine healers must always fight."

When she's not writing books, giving readings, or appearing on television, Browne devotes her time to several causes and charitable organizations, especially AIDS research. For the police, she volunteers her time to help locate missing children and solve crimes.

It's all in line with the underlying philosophy of the highly religious Browne, who includes prayer in all of her books. For Browne, there is nothing more powerful or remarkable in the universe than God, who is there for people whether or not they choose to acknowledge him. "It doesn't matter if you believe in God," she says, "because God believes in you."

C

Count Alesandro di Cagliostro
(a.k.a. Giuseppe Balsamo)
Healer, Mystic, Alchemist
(1743–1795)

O! he sits high in all the people's hearts;
And that which would appear offence in us,
His countenance, like richest alchemy,
Will change to virtue and to worthiness.
　　　　　—William Shakespeare, *Julius Caesar*

Count Alesandro di Cagliostro influenced, at times inspired, and other times, absolutely enraged the famous and influential. Catherine the Great hated him and Marie Antoinette barely tolerated him in spite of her husband's incessant fascination with the calculating count; the Prince of Wales embraced him, metaphorically speaking, of course, with two welcoming arms, until he ran afoul of the prince's favor; William Blake and Johann Goethe wrote about him; he also appears in Alexandre Dumas's *Memoirs of a Physician*, in Thomas Carlyle's *Miscellanies*, and as Sarastro in Wolfgang Mozart's *The Magic Flute*. He even comes up again, this time as himself, as played by Orson Welles, in *Black Magic*, a film made more than 150 years after his death.

The world's most lovingly hated charmer chameleon, Cagliostro was as fleet of foot as he was quick of tongue. He was the ultimate successful rogue; a deliciously dastardly cad who lived on his wits, subsisting on a diet of pure ingenuity, an uncanny ability of falling into favor with influential people, and an extraordinary knack for fraud and forgery. And while his psychic "abilities" were dubious at best, he had so many devoted believers and followers, it's hard to believe that he was a total sham.

Sicilian-born into poverty in Palermo on June 8, 1743, as Giuseppe Balsamo, Cagliostro's father died when he was very young and his mother sent him away to live with his uncle, a fairly established and successful jeweler, because she didn't have the means to support her young son.

His uncle was dictatorial and the household oppressive, so he ran away and often. The last time he fled, he got caught and was henceforth sent to live at the Benedictine monastery of Caltagirone in Sicily. Briefly educated there, he began to become interested in science and medicine, and may have gone on to become a doctor, but his free spirit and wild side always seemed to get the better of him. When he was seventeen, he discovered alchemy, and that was almost enough to keep him in his studies, but he also knew the world was full of opportunities for learning more about this mysterious science and God only knew what else.

Soon, experiencing much the same pinch on his "wings" among the monks, he fell in with a rough crowd, getting into as much trouble as he could find. He was nearly expelled for his misconduct many times and all but disowned by most of his shamed family, though his ever-patient uncle continued to extricate him from the complex jams he typically landed in and kept him out of jail.

Eventually, he fled from the monastery and decided to travel the world. While in Malta, he changed his name, giving himself the noble title of "count." Also in Malta, he fell in good standing with the grand master of the Maltese Order, who, himself, was also a practicing alchemist.

Soon, the travel bug bit him again and he was off.

He traveled to Greece and learned more about alchemy. He discovered the Freemasons; he took to them and they also strongly took to him. As a Freemason, he used his connections to forge a trail throughout Europe, and then throughout Egypt, Arabia, Persia, Rhodes, India, and Ethiopia, all the while voraciously taking in everything he could absorb about alchemy and the occult. To gain more influence—and, of course, meals and lodging—he fabricated tons of tales, including that he had been initiated into the Sovereign Military Order of the Knights of Malta.

Soon enough, Cagliostro was touting himself as a healer and alchemist, and he continued his travels. When he learned he could prey on people's grief from loss, he added an ability to hear the dead to his resume, and he conducted numerous séances. Records disagree as to whether he was truly clairaudient. While he didn't believe himself to be anything more than a faker, he made a lot of successful communication in his séances—on purpose or not.

In the late 1760s, while traveling through Rome, he met his future wife, Lorenza Feliciani, in whom he had found a most complementary accomplice. Lorenza was an artisan's daughter and tired of the stability and predictability of her life, so she took off with and married the count, calling herself Countess Serafina, and became his assistant on his exploits.

The maniacal newlyweds traveled together, dazzling whoever they could with their "magical" abilities, selling bogus youth elixirs, beauty fixers, and alchemist powders. Cagliostro continued his fantastic fabrications, captivating people with his magic and making them believe obvious fallacies, like that he was a thousand years old and remembered watching the pyramids being built.

In London in early to mid-1770s, he met the Comte de St.-Germain, who introduced him to Egyptian Freemasonry. Cagliostro took it one step further and installed himself as grand copt of the order of Egyptian Masonry, organizing lodges in England, Germany, Russia, and France.

The count and countess finally settled down for a while in Paris in 1772, where they peddled more of their elixirs and powders, conducted séances, and kept themselves busy. For Cagliostro, his popularity grew just as it had with any other psychic: people either liked or disliked him; he acquired believers who worshipped him and gave whatever they had—their money, their influence, their reputations, and even their lives—to keep him out of the prisons in which the skeptics so wished he'd die and rot away.

Eventually, Cagliostro managed to ingratiate himself into the court of Louis XVI. It was the same as ever: He was staunchly disliked by some, and adored and revered by others. But it didn't amount to anything what anyone else thought of him: the king loved him and that's all that mattered.

That is, until a stolen necklace caused him to fall out of favor in 1785.

In a kind of prelude to the forthcoming French Revolution, Madame LaMotte had perpetrated a scheme to implicate the queen. She convinced the unsuspecting Cardinal Rohan to act as an "agent" for the king in obtaining a diamond necklace for Marie Antoinette, who as of late, had been turning off her husband. King Louis XVI had, in fact, issued no such order; in fact, the necklace the poor cardinal had been commissioned to obtain was actually stolen, and, when it was found out, the scheme horribly backfired.

By this time already falling out of favor with His Majesty, Cagliostro was suspected of involvement in the scam and was imprisoned for six months. He was released from prison when he went to trial and talked his way out of being implicated, confusing the court with his defense until no connection could firmly be made between him and the scam.

Whether he was truly innocent or guilty is not known; what is known, however, is that he was banished from France for good. So he fled to London, where he got himself into more trouble, and then fled again.

In 1789, Cagliostro headed back to Rome with Lorenza. When he tried to establish a Masonic lodge in the unforgivingly Catholic city, he sealed his doom. The ongoing Inquisition got him on charges of heresy, conjury, magic, and freemasonry and chucked him into prison in 1791. He was originally handed a death sentence, but he managed to wriggle his way out of that one, somehow having his sentence commuted by the presiding pope.

Lorenza, who had turned on Cagliostro, was sent to live out her days in a convent. Cagliostro, himself, died in a dungeon in the prison of San Leo on August 26, 1795.

Edgar Cayce

Prophet, Healer

(1877–1945)

According to many teachings, the subconscious is the realm of the soul that uses the conscious mind as a

COURTESY OF A.R.E.

*mechanism for manifesting in the physical plane
through the five senses. Often, the thoughts and
interests of the conscious mind, coupled with the
desires of the body, become so strong and dominant
that only its activities seem important and real; the
subconscious seems illusionary and unrelated to outer
life. But in truth, the real life is occurring in the
subconscious.*

—Edgar Cayce

If there's any generality that can be made about psychic phenomena, aside from its connections to religion, it's that it is closely tied both to the teachings and acceptance of the philosophies of the

East and to the New Age movement. Through her psychic visions and teachings, Madame Blavatsky (see page 35) first introduced Eastern philosophy to Western consciousness. But it is Edgar Cayce (pronounced CAY-see) to whom is now attributed the moniker "Father of the New Age." His prophecies, diagnoses, and prescriptions led to a new way of thinking: that illness and healing were linked to the mind as much as to the body.

For more than forty years, the "sleeping prophet" closed his eyes, dozed off, and then, given the name of a person either in the room or not, known to him or not, he would pinpoint ailments without having to be told in advance what they were and provide a prescription for relief. The ethereal examination would end with Cayce saying, "We are through."

It certainly goes without saying that Cayce astounded medical practitioners and regular folks alike. He always knew how unusual his gift was and how unlikely it was that he would have been the one who received it. Still, he accepted it and tried to explain it to those who could not.

The crux of Cayce's message lies in this:

The great paradox of humankind is that we are both spirit and flesh. That's like saying we're a combination of oil and water, two substances which do not combine. . . . How can anything be made up of two substances that are impossible to combine? Yet, such is the nature of humanity. We are constantly forced to reconcile the seemingly irreconcilable: mercy with justice, cooperation with independence, unity with diversity, tradition with change, feeling with thought, love with truth, and on and on.

With that, he gave substance and meaning to the miracles he seemed to perform.

Edgar Cayce was born into farm life in Hopkinsville, Kentucky, on March 18, 1877, the lone brother of four sisters. There was always a huge extended family of uncles, aunts, and cousins buzzing about, but while he was always surrounded by people, he still managed to have imaginary friends. Even as a young child, Cayce had visions of dead relatives with whom he carried on endless conversations; his family chalked up these visions to "fertile imagination" and all but ignored them.

Cayce was barely educated, but he cherished the Bible. And while he didn't generally concern himself with reading, this was a book he went through cover to cover at least once a year. He took much solace in its messages and the Good Book guided and influenced him for the rest of his life. Even when he began to accept his supernatural powers, the Bible and Christian teachings affected him. Some of his most controversial beliefs, like reincarnation, which he faced for the first time as late as 1923, weren't part of the message of the Bible, but he was able to rectify his new beliefs with the understanding that "[d]eath is only passing through God's other door" and that "[a]ll souls were created in the beginning and are finding their way back from whence they came."

At age thirteen, he had a vision that shaped his destiny: He was playing in a field, minding his own business, and out of nowhere, a woman appeared to him. She asked him what he wanted out of life. Growing up, Cayce dreamed of becoming a medical missionary, and so he told the woman that he wanted to help people. In his life, he had realized that childhood dream and remained true to the pledge he made to the woman in his vision, whom he considered to be an angel.

The biggest obstacle to Cayce becoming a medical missionary, however, was that he was never much of a student. Shortly after his vocational angel vision, however, he made a startling discovery. By falling asleep on top of his homework one night, he learned he could photographically absorb all the contents of a book just by sleeping on it. It was a revelation—and where his understanding of greater consciousness through unconsciousness took root.

When Cayce was old enough to leave home, he moved to the city, making a living as a salesman, a career he realized he was suited to, and one in which he found great success. But then, in 1901, a case of severe laryngitis that lasted more than a year ended his career. He went to countless doctors, but no one could cure his unusual illness.

When one door closes, another opens, and because he could no longer be an effective salesman, he turned his attention to photography and made an equally successful living at that.

He didn't know it then, but another door was about to close, and another would be opening.

Around that time, hypnotism was becoming very big, and a traveling hypnotist just happened to stop in Cayce's town. Curious, Cayce went to one of the demonstrations and was himself hypnotized. Eerily enough, when Cayce was under hypnosis, he spoke in a normal voice, confirming that nothing was physically wrong with him.

Several weeks later, Al Layne, a local self-trained hypnotist who had seen the demonstration and was intrigued by what had transpired with the young photographer, convinced Cayce to go under with him. Again, Cayce began to speak in a normal voice. But there was more this time. Hypnotized, Cayce diagnosed his condition as a "psychological condition producing a physical effect" and then named his cure. When he awoke, Layne explained to him what had happened and Cayce decided to give his prescription a try. He was right and he got his voice back.

It was a case of "mind over matter," a phenomenon not as commonly known then as it is today. The connection between wellness of mind and wellness of body was made by Cayce, so he decided to dabble in getting to the bottom of this connection and started to give readings as early as 1901. He wasn't entirely confident in this, however. Awake, he still knew nothing about medicine or even anatomy, even though asleep, he was as learned and influential as Hippocrates himself. He was understandably fearful that he was not educated or a doctor; his faith made him believe he could help.

Hypnotism was exhausting and it took a huge toll on him, so he decided to give it up and stick with photography. But when Cayce made a helpful diagnosis for his friend Layne, who had been suffering stomach problems, he decided to consent to experiments, as he clearly had a gift for helping others. However, he would stop the experimentation if he put anyone in any kind of danger.

While all this was going on, his personal life also started to improve. He had met Gertrude Evans in 1897 and promised to marry her when he was established enough in his career to raise a family. They were finally married in 1903 and moved to Bowling Green, Kentucky, to start their life together. A son, Hugh Lynn, was born in 1907.

Cayce still considered himself a photographer first, even though he had begun to make a name for himself in the psychic business, which had also proved to be more lucrative. Fate intervened when not one but two of his photography studios burned down, leaving him in an insurmountable hole of debt. The photography door slammed firmly and effectively shut in his face, and he devoted more time to using his psychic talents, though he did not give up photography altogether. Not yet, at least.

Cayce was making a name for himself, and even the skeptics had to concede when, in 1910, Cayce was legitimized by a doctor's article published in the October 9, 1910, *New York Times*; "Illiterate Man Becomes a Doctor When Hypnotized." Cayce had treated the reporter who broke the story, and, like many whom Cayce would convert, he became a firm believer for life. The miracles continued, and Cayce enjoyed world renown for his uncanny deliveries of cures. Still, he remained remarkably humble. "I do not claim to possess anything that other individuals do not inherently possess," he said. "I do not believe there is a single individual who does not possess this same ability I have."

And then tragedy struck again.

In 1911, Gertrude gave birth to their second son, Milton Porter. The baby was not healthy and died shortly after he was born. Cayce was angry that he had not tried to diagnose his son and do something to cure him.

The death was devastating to Cayce, but it nearly destroyed Gertrude. Shortly after the baby died, she fell extremely ill with tuberculosis. Doctors said her illness was terminal and that it would only be a matter of months before she was gone. Not willing to lose another loved one, this time Cayce intervened. He made his own diagnosis and implemented the treatment. Within a few days, she was feeling better; within months, she was fully recovered. Shortly after, Hugh Lynn was blinded by an illness. Cayce stepped in and cured his son as well.

By the mid-1920s, Cayce gave up photography altogether and embraced his calling as a psychic diagnostician. Determined to help as many people as he could—both by healing them and by teaching others to discover and nurture their own psychic healing abilities—he set out to build a hospital that would treat based on his diagnoses.

In 1928, the Edgar Cayce Hospital opened in Virginia Beach, Virginia. In 1929, he established the Atlantic University to teach New Age concepts and healing. Unfortunately, this venture folded during the Great Depression. What was established around the same time, in 1931, and which thrives even to the present day, was his Association for Research and Enlightenment, Inc. (ARE), in Virginia Beach. More than 70,000 visitors flock to ARE every year to learn about Cayce's life and teachings, as well as to partake in what is still one of the group's most famous offerings: ESP testing.

To this day, skeptics try to prove Cayce to be little more than a talented manipulator of minds. In a fairly recent article in the *Skeptical Inquirer*, Dale Beyerstein labels Cayce's talent as "subjective validation"—people wanted to believe he was right, so they believed. Not all skeptics remain disbelievers, however. Many were and continue to be converted.

Cayce was active and devoted to helping others throughout his life, but World War II took its toll on him. So eager was he to help people that he all but exhausted himself with his effort. He suffered a minor stroke and developed edema of the lungs. When he collapsed in 1944, he called it quits in the psychic diagnostician arena.

In September 1944, Cayce gave his final reading—and it was about him and his failing health. Then, on New Year's Day, 1945, he said he would be buried on January 5. He died on January 3 and was buried, as predicted, two days later. Gertrude followed him to the other side a few months later, on Easter Sunday.

Cayce's accomplishments are many and vast. In addition to his medical advances, he also made many prophecies. In trance, he predicted the stock market crash of 1929, as well as the end of the Great Depression. He predicted both world wars and the deaths of Presidents Franklin Delano Roosevelt, whom he outlived in his lifetime, and John F. Kennedy, who wouldn't even be in office for fifteen years after Cayce's death. Of course, as is the case with many prophecies, sometimes one must stretch the meaning to fit the event. "Ye are to have turmoils—ye are to have strife between capital and labor," is how the prophecy actually read. "Ye are to have a division in thy own land, before ye have the second of the Presidents that next will not live through his office." He never actually named anyone specifically, or what that "division in thy own land" would be. Perhaps he meant the growing rift between the Republican and Democratic parties, but the meaning is open to interpretation.

Some of the things Cayce predicted haven't happened, including the one picked up by at least five later psychics in this book alone: namely, the great global change caused by the shift of the earth's axis. He said this would occur in 2001; as that date got closer, Ruth Montgomery (see page 175), years after Cayce's death, gave the message from her spirit guides (who may have included Cayce, but it's not certain) that the shift was still going to occur, but in 2012. Others hold true to this 2012 date.

One prediction Cayce made that has not yet come to pass is the uncovering of the great "Hall of Records" left by survivors of Atlantis. He predicted that this was going to happen between 1996 and 1998, and it would be linked to the Second Coming of Christ. He was also convinced that Atlantis itself, which he estimated was about the size "of Europe, including Asia in Europe," would rise out of the sea in 1968 or 1969.

In trance, Cayce could speak in two dozen foreign languages. And he did provide answers to ancient mysteries that archaeologists had been able to prove after his death. By the time he was through, Cayce had given more than 14,000 readings on more than 10,000 different subjects.

Cayce's message can be summed up in a simple statement: Meditation equals being closer to God, which equals health and happiness. As Cayce said, "All strength, all healing of every nature is the changing of vibrations from within, the attuning of the divine within the living tissue of a body to Creative Energies. This alone is healing. Whether it is accomplished by the use of drugs, the knife, or what not, it is the attuning of the atomic structure of the living force to its spiritual heritage."

LIBRARY OF CONGRESS

Aleister Crowley
Mystic
(1875–1947)

His reputation had been that of a man who worshipped Satan, but it was more accurately said that he worshipped no one except himself.

—Leading skeptic author Martin Gardner, of Aleister Crowley

The self-proclaimed "wickedest man on earth," Aleister Crowley had a huge presence in the occult, while he lived and even in the present day. He called himself many nefarious names, including the Antichrist, the Beast of Revelations, and just simply 666.

Crowley was a contemporary of Grigori Rasputin's (see page 193), although he lived much longer. However, in looking at both their lives, a neat parallel can be drawn to both men in the way they conducted themselves. Rasputin believed that through sinning and excessive behavior, he could get closer to God; Crowley wasn't interested in getting closer to God, per se. Unless you take the point of view that Crowley had possibly thought of himself as a kind of god—because if nothing else, he was in it for himself.

Crowley's most famous book, *The Book of the Law* (1904), outlines his premise for living. He advocated a way of life he called "the Law of Thelema." The word "thelema" is Greek for "the will," and that's what Crowley was all about. He writes, "Do what thou wilt shall be the whole of the law/Love is the law, law under will/Every man and every woman is a star." In a lifetime that spanned more than seventy years, the out and in-your-face drug-using, bisexual, sex fiend, mind-manipulating Crowley, after believing he had received a vision telling him how he was to live, made this his own personal creed, especially the first part of it, and it didn't matter to him how many people got squashed in the process.

It's no revelation that oppressively religious upbringings often produce reactionary adults. Whether these children grow into adults who are ready to accept, embrace, and take even further everything they have been taught, or if they take the absolute opposite tack to do anything they can to break free from their soul shackles is up to the individual.

Crowley grew up in one such religiously oppressive household. Born October 12, 1875, into a family of fanatical Christians, in Leamington Spa, an area of Warwickshire, Crowley hated the strict Victorian morality that defined his youth, which he blamed, for the most part, on his father. The family belonged to a particularly strict sect of Christianity known as Plymouth Brethren—if not the strictest.

Edward Alexander Crowley, the son of a wealthy and successful evangelical brewer, made it clear from an early age that he hated the moral code shoved down his throat, his affluence, and, especially, his father. So much did he despise the man, in fact, that he even changed the name his father gave him. Crowley rebelled constantly, setting off explosions and torturing animals, among his many evil antics.

Crowley's father passed away when he was eleven, and he could already feel that the strings that bound him to Christianity were beginning to fray and snap. By the time he was fourteen, he managed to lose his virginity to one of the maids in the house, thus sparking a sexual appetite that would prove insatiable throughout his life.

When he came of age, he came into a huge inheritance, which meant he never had to work a day in his life. Which also meant he had plenty of time to corrupt, sodomize, and enlighten.

Most of this started in 1895, when he began his studies at Cambridge. In 1896, he had his first mystical experience in Stockholm. "I was awakened to the knowledge that I possessed a magical means of becoming conscious and of satisfying a part of my nature which had up to that moment concealed itself from me," he later wrote. "It was an experience of horror and pain, combined with a certain ghostly terror, yet at the same time it was the key to the purest and holiest spiritual ecstasy that exists."

In 1898, at age twenty-three, Crowley joined the Golden Dawn, a permissive sect of the controversial Freemasons. He was initiated as Frater Perdurabo (Perdurabo is Latin for "I will endure") on November 18, 1898. His oppressively religious early years made the free and easy tenets of Golden Dawn, which were essentially a synthesis of kabbalah, alchemy, tarot, astrology, ritual magic, and more, even more appealing to the budding hedonist. In the Golden Dawn, he learned he could achieve enlightenment through study and knowledge, without worship. It was like a dream come true.

But the Golden Dawn didn't want Crowley anywhere near as much as he wanted it. In 1900, despite his enthusiasm, Golden Dawn members refused to promote him through their ranks for many reasons. His bisexual proclivities were only part of it. More pressing was that Crowley was an undeniably influential person, and, he was pretty evil. Basically, they were just darn scared of the ramifications of the havoc he might cause in the order should he advance to the top.

So after the controversy, he left the Golden Dawn and set off on a pilgrimage of sorts. Following in the footsteps of so many spiritual leaders before him, and to come, he traveled the world, soaking up bits of knowledge wherever he could to help him advance his own cause. And luckily, he still had a lot of that inheritance left to fund his quest.

He went to Mexico in 1900, where he wrote *Tannhauser and Alice: An Adultery*. He left Mexico and traveled through all the countries of the East. Ready to get back to Western culture, he headed back to Europe in 1902.

In Paris, that same year, he made the acquaintance of a yet unknown young author, Somerset Maugham. So overcome by Crowley was Maugham that he wrote one of his earliest novels, *The Magician*, based on Crowley, which he published in 1906. This is not the only place Crowley comes up in popular culture, to be sure. He had a huge influence on musicians especially. Years after his death, his face appeared on the cover of the Beatles' *Sgt. Pepper's Lonely Hearts Club Band* album. Ozzy Osbourne wrote a song about him. And Led Zeppelin's Jimmy Page bought Crowley's house.

Aside from "artist's muse," Crowley is widely known as a misogynistic maniac who literally ruined women: He was married twice, and both wives reportedly went insane. He also had five mistresses who killed themselves—not to mention a whole string of countless others who either drank or drugged themselves to death.

When Rose Kelly married Crowley in 1903, she had no idea what she was getting into. She was taken in by Crowley's smoothness and general verve, and while his true side likely began to surface early on, he probably was able to talk his way out of all kinds of sticky situations he caused.

Rose and Aleister had a daughter, Lola Zaza, who died from typhus in India while Crowley was away from his family in 1907. By 1909, he and Rose were divorced; his doing, and on claims that she was an alcoholic—no doubt having something to do with the death of their child? It didn't matter to him. There was pleasure to be had and now he was free to immerse himself in it.

After his divorce, Crowley began to develop a strong interest in reincarnation. He surmised that he spent his past lives as Count Cagliostro (see page 51) and Edward Talbott Kelley, who was an assistant to Dr. John Dee (see page 79), among others. He never presumed to have been a good soul in any past life: He always chose caddish con artists and those of that ilk.

In 1904, while still married to Rose, who was herself a known clairvoyant, Crowley published his seminal work *Book of the Law*, which he claimed was dictated to him by Aiwass, essentially his "guardian angel," whom he had "encountered" during a visit to Cairo. He published several more books, including *Book of Lies* (1913), *Diary of a Drug Fiend* (1922), and *Equinox of the Gods* (1937).

Of these, the history behind *Drug Fiend* is probably the most interesting, as it brings out the humanity Crowley never quite accepted was part of him. Remarried and set up in the Abbey of Thelema in Sicily, Crowley was heavily addicted to heroin, as was his wife. The "novel" is a story about a couple living through the addiction with happier results than what had actually transpired.

At the abbey, his second daughter died. When a Crowley disciple also died at the abbey, the cause of death unknown, the disciple's wife went back to London to expose Crowley in the papers as a practitioner of black magic. In 1923, a rising, raging Benito Mussolini kicked him out of Italy; in 1929, he was also banished from France under similar circumstances.

It was downhill all the way from there. By 1935, he was bankrupt. He died, alone, on December 1, 1947, still addicted to heroin and essentially a mess. His last words reportedly were "I am perplexed."

After his death, the Aleister Crowley Foundation was established to keep alive and to promote the teachings of Thelema. Many, even more than fifty years after Crowley's death, continue to see his message as one by which to live and keep Crowley's legacy active and flourishing.

In a comprehensive biography of Crowley published in 2001, author Lawrence Sutin sums up the life and contributions of Aleister Crowley to society, "[He] was at his best when pointing the way to diligent individual effort, and at his worst when purporting to govern his fellows and to forecast the course of history."

D

Andrew Jackson Davis
(a.k.a. "The Poughkeepsie Seer")
Clairvoyant, Seer
(1826–1910)

> *It is a truth that spirits commune with one another
> while one is in the body and the other in the higher
> spheres—and this, too, when the person in the body is
> unconscious of the influx, and hence cannot be
> convinced of the fact; and this truth will ere long
> present itself in the form of a living demonstration.
> And the world will hail with delight the ushering in of
> that era when the interiors of men will be opened, and
> the spiritual communion will be established.*
>
> —Andrew Jackson Davis's prediction
> of the coming modern spiritualist
> movement, as presented in his
> *Principles of Nature* (1847)

Andrew Jackson Davis is to the modern spiritualism movement as dawn is to the day. Prophet indeed, it was Davis who predicted and proclaimed that modern spiritualism was on its way. In his career, Davis wrote over thirty books about spiritualism and essentially set the ball in motion for those who followed.

The much touted "father of modern spiritualism" was born in Blooming Grove, New York, on August 11, 1826. He grew up as poor as a Dickensian street urchin. His mother, Elizabeth, nee Robinson, Davis was uneducated and unavailable; his father, Samuel, was first and foremost a raving alcoholic, a weaver and shoemaker second. Davis, thus, had to work most of his young life, depriving him of an education he so sorely craved. In his life, Davis wanted more than anything else to be a doctor; it would be many years before he would make that dream a reality for himself. There was other work to be done first.

Even as a young child, Davis began having visions. When he was eleven or twelve, he experienced one so vivid, it compelled him to convince his father that the family had to move to the larger town of Poughkeepsie, New York, and right away. Samuel, possibly drunk at the time, decided it made perfect sense to uproot the family based on a vision his young son had, so they packed up and settled in their new life by 1838. His mother died when he was still a boy; his father never improved and was soon in the grave himself.

In the early 1840s, twenty-five or so years after the death of its inventor, Franz Anton Mesmer, hypnotism was starting to catch on. As a result, hypnotists began traveling around the country like circus acts. It was an infectious concept that thoughts could be seduced from the subconscious, and many were curious to see it in action.

Among the curious was Davis, so in 1843, when Davis was about seventeen, he jumped on the chance to check it out. Dr. J. S. Grimes, one of the top hypnotists of the day, was making a stop in Poughkeepsie. Excitedly, Davis went to get himself hypnotized. But it didn't take. He didn't disavow it all together; he just waned in enthusiasm for a while.

When given the opportunity to be hypnotized months later by a local self-trained tailor named William Levingston, he wholeheartedly accepted. After being put in a trance by the talented tailor, Davis had a pre–Edgar Cayce (see page 61) experience: he learned that he had the ability to see right through the human body with his "spirit eyes." These he felt at the middle of his forehead, and through them, he felt he could diagnose medical disorders. So for a while, he could live out his doctoring dream, aiding the sick and curing their ills.

But that wasn't what caused him to realize his unusual powers;

his initiation to the psychic world would be much more dramatic than that.

On a regular night in March 1844, Davis fell into a trance. During this trance, he claimed that he was infused with incredible psychic power that allowed him to fly all the way from Poughkeepsie to the Catskill Mountains, some forty miles north—and all within the same night. After arriving at his destination, he was greeted by Swedish philosopher Emanuel Swedenborg (see page 202), who years before had lain the groundwork for spiritualism through his direct conversations with the angels and with Jesus himself, and by the ancient Greek physician Galen.

Reportedly, Galen gave Davis a magical staff for healing, and Swedenborg promised to guide him in his future psychic work. Essentially, their message to him was that it was time to share his psychic powers with the world. Fully believing in them and the profound experience he had had, he readily complied.

After making his way back to Poughkeepsie after his astral adventure, Davis put a plan in place. He started out small, just in his small town, really, but soon enough, he was traveling extensively and giving lectures. He allowed himself to be hypnotized many times, and, in those sessions, he espoused knowledge he could not possibly ever have known with such a limited education and a life spent experiencing little more than the small-town offerings of Poughkeepsie.

In 1845, he began dictating, in trance, his great work, *The Principles of Nature: Her Divine Revelations and a Voice to Mankind*, which, among other concepts, illuminated the power of the psychic universe and all it had to offer if one made him- or herself open to it.

What is almost as colorful as Davis's psychic life was his married life—or lives, to be more accurate. Davis had been known to break up many marriages, including his own, and got hitched three times.

Married for the first time at the age of twenty-two, Davis's wife, Catherine de Wolf, was already in her forties. When they met, she was only separated from her husband, but meeting Davis was the push she needed to finalize her divorce. Sadly, she was ill even when they married in 1848; she died on November 2, 1853. After her death, he wrote about several visitations she paid him as "Cylonia," and even referred to her as such, never again uttering her living name.

Barely a year later, in 1854, he met another soon-to-be divorcée, Mary Fenn Robinson, who was only two years older than him. They were married in 1855.

Thirty years later, it was time for Davis to break up another marriage—two to be exact. This time, one was his own. Davis filed for divorce to marry the already-married-twice-and-now-on-the-way-to-divorce-number-two, younger-by-thirteen-years Delphine "Della" Elizabeth Markham. They were married in August that same year.

In the early 1880s, now financially able to realize his dream of becoming a medical doctor, he attended the U.S. Medical College in New York. (It was here that he met Delphine.) He got his degree in 1883 and he and Delphine moved to Boston. There, he practiced medicine and ran the Progressive Bookstore. When he retired from medicine, he continued to run the bookshop until his death on January 13, 1910.

In March 1848, Davis recorded a prescient entry in his diary, "About daylight this morning a war breathing passed over my face and I heard a voice, tender and strong, saying, 'Brother, the good work has begun—behold a living demonstration is born.' I was left wondering what could be meant by such a message." That night, not so far away from where Davis was in New York state, the Fox sisters sparked the modern spiritualist movement by communicating with the spirit of a dead peddler, who had been killed and buried in the house in which they lived (see page 120).

Davis would live to see its birth and its struggles—and also to see Maggie Fox condemn it publicly and also to rescind her condemnation. He would be dead more than ten years when spiritualism got a revival in the 1920s, when Mina Crandon (see page 165), more commonly known as Margery the Medium, made her work public in Boston, the same city in which he lived the last years of his life and died.

John Dee

Astrologer, Occultist, Angel Communicator
(1527–1608)

> Now I want
> Spirits to enforce, art to enchant,
> And my ending is despair,
> Unless I be relieved by prayer,
> Which pierces so that it assaults
> Mercy itself and frees all faults.
> As you from crimes would pardon'd be,
> Let your indulgence set me free.
>> —Prospero, a character based on Dr. John Dee,
>> from William Shakespeare's *The Tempest*

John Dee was a gifted mathematician and scholar who lived during the time of William Shakespeare; in fact, so famous was Dee for his talents that Shakespeare himself immortalized him in his plays, basing the characters Prospero from *The Tempest* and King Lear on the noted scholar. What he is most remembered for, however, is his communication with angels and the unfortunate fallout he had with polite society over his interest in alchemy.

When he was respected, he was glorified. Dee owned a library of more than 4,000 books, rivaling in size any personal library in Renaissance England. He was extremely well educated. Among his many miscellaneous accomplishments, he coined the term "Britannia." He is known as the founder of the Rosicrucian Order, a sect of protestant "Jesuits." He is also credited with putting a hex on the Spanish Armada. But however book smart he was, street smart he was not, and that flaw would eventually do him in.

Born in Mortlake, a small village on the Thames, outside of London, Dee was an academic superstar, dazzling his parents and teachers as a gifted and driven student. He was accepted at St. John's College in Cambridge at age fifteen, where he claimed to study an astounding eighteen hours a day. In 1546, he was appointed under-reader of Greek at Trinity College and shortly thereafter was made a fellow.

At Trinity, Dee experienced his first taste of persecution for his actions. This had nothing to do with his later interest in the occult, but more for his mastery of science. For a school production of Aristophanes' *Pax*, Dee constructed a mechanical beetle as a prop that was so terrifyingly lifelike, he faced charges of sorcery and expulsion. He was promptly kicked out of Trinity and reviled by the court of Queen Mary. Essentially, he had to leave England.

Dee headed to Belgium in 1547. There, he befriended a cartographer, Geradus Mercator. Coming back to England a couple of years later, he brought back with him globes that Mercator had, well, not necessarily *given* him. It has been said that it is more like he took them, smuggling them into his own country to try and look good to the queen.

Elizabeth I, when she came to power, made Dee a favorite of her court. He presented her with the globes that he had brought back with him, and with these, he impressed her by showing her all the territories that Britain could conquer and by plotting maps. The queen took a shine to the young academic, protecting him and even giving him money throughout his life. He even plotted her star chart for her, earning him the distinction of "the royal astrologer." He also advised her in matters of the occult, a subject of much intrigue to the young, curious queen.

Also in the 1550s, Dee began to be intrigued by the prospect of natural magic, both white and black. He was more interested in white magic, however. Although he felt a certain natural affinity for magic, the logician in him didn't allow him to completely trust his own abilities; therefore, he depended on others to help him in his psychic work, which, in part, led to somewhat disastrous consequences.

Among the very bad "street stupid" choices he made was in those he enlisted to help him explore the secrets of the supernatural realm and the concepts of telepathy, spiritualism, crystal gazing, and dream interpretation. His first assistant, Barnabas Saul, didn't last very long. Dee was tipped off pretty early on that Saul, working in the interest of Dee's detractors, had ingratiated himself with Dee in order to trip him up and bring him down.

Eventually, Dee hired a second assistant. In 1582, he took the younger-by-thirty-years Edward Talbott Kelley under his wing and into his work. Dee suspected that Kelley was probably not going to be looking after Dee's best interests, even writing in his diary, "I know this man is a bit of a rogue, but he has been through the mill, so to speak." Kelley was a ne'er do well, but Dee thought he deserved a second chance at life. And Dee didn't regret bringing Kelley on—at least at first. It was through working with Kelley that Dee's most memorable work began.

Through scrying and with the help of Kelley's mediumistic talents,

Dee could have conversations with the angels, whom he called "scholemasters." The angels were not interested in Kelley at all; the young medium merely pulled them through into the physical realm, but it was Dee who communicated with them and translated what they said for the world at large. According to author Deborah E. Harkness, Dee "communicated with a dizzying array of angels during his conversations, both well-known and obscure, all of whom possessed individual personalities, appearances, and demeanours."

Dee's techniques for talking with angels made up something called the Enchain Language, which is still in use to work with angels today. He left behind diaries that showed his belief that it was necessary to communicate with angels to reform natural philosophy because they were the messengers of God's plans. The angels told Dee all about the lands that the British Empire would conquer and more.

Although his association with Kelley opened the door for him to be able to communicate with the angels, what Dee himself felt was his greatest accomplishment, it also led him down several frowned-upon avenues, including alchemy, which caused him to be all but shunned by the nobles who once embraced him. Reportedly, Elizabeth never lost her affection for her favorite astrologer and occult expert—but kept him at arms' length, not giving him nearly as much support or money as she had before. The great Dr. John Dee died broke and alone in 1608.

The Delphic Oracle

Prophets, Seers

(1400 B.C.E.–392 C.E.)

They say that the seat of the oracle is a cavern
hollowed deep down in the earth, with a rather

narrow mouth, from which rises a pneuma *that
produces divine possession. A tripod is set above this
cleft, mounting which, the Pythia inhales the vapor
and prophesises.*

—Strabo (64/63 B.C.E.–23 C.E.), ancient Greek
geographer and historian

The Delphic Oracle was not one priest or priestess, but many
women, of various ages and economic statuses. These women,
the "Pythia," were trained to speak the Greek god Apollo's messages. One didn't have to come from noble lineage to assume this
prestigious position; all that was required was a long, intensive training period and, above all, purity and abstinence from sexual activity,
as well as, in some cases, fasting.

How did it work? Once properly trained and primed for her duty,
the Pythia would enter the *adyton*, a kind of chasm that existed
within the temple of Apollo in Delphi, at Mount Parnassus. There,
she acted in silence, with pure thoughts, and waited for the power to
overtake her as she breathed in the vapors, referred to throughout the
literature as "pneuma." Sometimes she even drank the water that
gave off the vapors. These women, spurred by the powers of the
vapors, would fall into trances, through which they would be able to
relay messages from Apollo himself to whomever asked.

Not only did the Pythia have to be pure; visitors, having paid
their fee, were directed to a sacred fountain, where they would wash
before they would be brought to the special chasm. There, sitting
on a golden stool with a tripod base, the Pythia would begin to
chant and sing. Her chantings would then be translated by a priest
of the temple. Once her message was delivered, she would be completely exhausted and out of breath.

Visitors famous and common alike abounded to the shrine to
learn their varied fates. Commoners asked questions about crops and
their villages. Generals looked to the oracle to strategize battles.
Famous visitors to the oracle included Plato and Alexander the Great.

Plutarch, who had surmised that the oracle was beginning to lose its potency when he was installed as one of two priests of the temple of Apollo, described the relationship as the Pythia acting as a musical instrument in the hands of the musician, Apollo. Says Plutarch, "The prophetic priestesses are moved [by the god] each in accordance with her natural facilities. . . . As a matter of fact, the voice is not that of a god . . . but all these are the woman's; [Apollo] puts into her mind only the visions, and creates a light in her soul in regard to the future."

The odor of the pneuma could be detected by anyone and it reportedly smelled like sweet perfume; however, it could not induce trance in anyone but the Pythia. Whatever it really was that gave the Pythia her prophetic powers, the messages of the classical clairvoyants were essentially taken on faith, perpetuated through legend, and immortalized in literature.

In literature and legend, many reportedly sought out advice from the oracle, and the news wasn't always good. In *The Oresteia*, Orestes learns that he will kill his mother, Clytemnestra, to avenge her murder of his father, Agamemnon. He won't accept it; first that his mother will kill his father and second that he will kill his own mother, but yet the tragedy unfolds. And in the Oedipus trilogy, it was the Delphic Oracle that prophesied to Jocasta that her son would murder her husband, Laius, and then marry her. After learning this unthinkable prediction, Jocasta abandons her infant son in the mountains. Later, Laius is slain by an unidentified man who thinks Laius is a robber. Arriving in Crete, the mystery man becomes a hero and takes the widow Jocasta's hand, neither knowing they are mother and son, and the prophecy is fulfilled.

Whatever it was that really gave the Pythia her powers in that chasm was not ever questioned; her authority never came under scrutiny. Regardless, the temple was closed and destroyed in the 390s, at the behest of the Christian Emperor Theodosis.

In modern times, curiosity about the temple and the oracle arose once again. As reported in a recent article in *Scientific American* called "Questioning the Delphic Oracle," at the turn of the twentieth century excavations began to take place at Delphi to uncover the exact location of the chasm to gain modern insight into the "miracle" of the pneuma vapors. The excavations continued for years, but no chasm was found in the temple.

The conclusion was reached that there was no chasm in the temple; and if there ever was, it would be impossible for any kind of natural gas to provoke the Pythia to her visions. This theory continued to be supported by scientists and archaeologists throughout the century, until the 1990s. At that time, a group of scientists put their facts together and were able to conclude by observing active faults in Greece that a chasm may in fact have existed at the site and that there may have been something in the gaseous emanations that could invoke trance. In 1996, another exploration determined that there was an area of Apollo's temple in Delphi in which a chasm may have existed. They discovered what they concluded to be the "oracle site," a place through which springs may very well have run. It was speculated that the gas emitted may have been carbon dioxide; however, there was still nothing found that could conclusively induce trance or hallucination.

Later, after more exploration and investigation, it was determined that limestone, prevalent in the area, when heated, could release petrochemical gases. Tests run on the water of the springs of Delphi showed traces of methane, ethylene, and ethane—essentially paint thinner—which, when inhaled, could cause a person to hallucinate. But whether it was hallucinations provoked by the inhalation of the gases, or the "voice" of Apollo speaking to the Pythia, the Delphic Oracle remains a psychic legend and mystery.

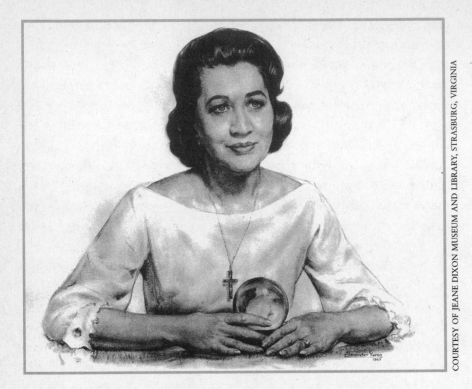

Jeane Dixon

Prophet, Astrologer

(1918–1997)

When asked to explain my gift for seeing the future,
I tell my questioners I could no more explain it than
I could really define love or electricity.

—Jeane Dixon

A Roman Catholic with a crystal ball—an impressive $8,000 crystal ball at that—who proclaimed that God was behind every prediction she ever made, Jeane Dixon is probably one of the best-known "pop psychics" who ever lived. Unwaveringly devoted to family and to protecting animal rights, Dixon made countless predictions—some of which came to pass, and, which is typically the case with psychic predictions, many of which did not.

Like Ruth Montgomery (see page 175), who wrote a best-selling book about Dixon, *A Gift of Prophecy* (1965), before going on to discover her own unique psychic powers, Dixon was based in Washington, D.C. Before her psychic life kicked off—and even afterward—Jeane made a living working with her husband in real estate. As she came into prominence, both celebrities and politicians came to rely on her promises and predictions. Sometimes, Dixon hit the mark; other times, she delivered news that people had wished they hadn't heard, and ignored, which proved unfortunately fatal for at least a couple of people. But we'll come back to that.

Born January 5, 1918, into a devout Catholic household, in Medford, Wisconsin, Jeane was raised in a family enjoying all the luxuries of upward mobility due to the success of an ever-expanding lumber company. They eventually moved to California, where Jeane had her first experience with a psychic. When she was eight years old, her mother took her to a fortune-teller who predicted the little girl would one day become a world-famous seer.

In 1939, she married James Dixon, who was an auto dealer with a budding interest in real estate. The couple moved to Washington, D.C., where they thrived in their real estate business and where Jeane first started to make the fortune-teller's prediction come true.

Between the connections the Dixons made in real estate and the success Jeane was having with her psychic abilities, the young couple was soon rubbing elbows with Washington's elite. In the early years, it has been reported that Jeane Dixon visited President Franklin Delano Roosevelt, and even advised him. Dixon's association with politicos didn't end with that administration, however. As late as the 1980s, she, among other psychics, had been commissioned by the First Lady, Nancy Reagan, to shed light on stuff about that presidency. Dixon was a very close friend of the late Senator Strom Thurmond for more than thirty years; she was the godmother of his son.

Jeane was the author of seven best-selling books, including *Astrology for Dogs* (1979) and an astrology cookbook.

During her career, Dixon is reported to have made prophecies with an accuracy rate of 60 percent. She had a pretty playful, matter-of-fact view on extrasensory perception, however. She once said, "I don't think telepathy will ever replace the telephone."

Among those things she predicted correctly was that Richard Nixon would become president and that China would become communist. She also predicted that Margaret Thatcher would become prime minister.

Tragically, Dixon is said to have predicted the untimely death of actress Carole Lombard. In January 1942, she had a vision that Lombard would perish in a plane crash and pleaded with the young star not to fly for a period of six weeks. Lombard, anxious to get back to her husband, Clark Gable, with whom she had just had a terrible spat, disregarded the warning. On Lombard's way back to California, within that six-week period, her plane ominously went down.

Another painful prediction saw the abrupt end of Camelot. In 1952, Dixon had foreseen that President John F. Kennedy would be elected. In the May 1956 issue of *Parade* magazine, she predicted he would "be assassinated or die in office." In November 1963, the eerie prophecy was fulfilled.

Dixon also foresaw the demise of another famous Kennedy, John's brother, Robert. When asked if he would become the next president, Dixon regretfully reported, in a lecture she was giving at the Ambassador Hotel, that "he will never become president of the United States because of a tragedy right here in this hotel."

For some of her predictions, however, it seems that she missed the mark. She guessed that Russia would be the first country to put a man on the Moon, and that World War III would begin in October 1958. In 1971, she surmised that "President Nixon would long be remembered for his courage . . ." and that he would be remembered as one of the all-time greatest presidents. This one is pretty subjective.

In more current events, she predicted George H. W. Bush would be reelected in 1992; that O.J. Simpson would be convicted in 1994 and "faces a long period of incarceration—until at least 1999"; that

Alec Baldwin would become nearly fatally ill in 1997; and that Ellen DeGeneres would crash the 1997 inauguration and have a run-in with the Secret Service.

A significant "incorrect prophecy"—or perhaps one not-yet-come-to-pass is reported in Montgomery's book:

> A child, born somewhere in the Middle East shortly after 7 A.M. (EST) on February 5, 1962, will revolutionize the world. Before the end of 1999 he will bring together all mankind in one all-embracing faith. This will be the foundation of a new Christianity, with every sect and creed united through this man who will walk among the people to spread the wisdom of the Almighty Power.

Jeane Dixon died on January 25, 1997, from a heart attack. A few months after her passing, Leo Bernstein, a close family friend, collected and stored some of Dixon's possessions and writings. A Jeane Dixon museum and library was created at the Wayside Foundation of American History and Arts, showcasing scrapbooks, essays, letters, and various personal effects and paying tribute to her life.

E

John Edward

Medium

(1970–)

I think that to prove [spirit contact] is a personal
thing. It is like saying, prove God. If you have
a belief system and you have faith, then there is
nothing really more than that.

—John Edward, to Larry King
on *Larry King Live,* 2001

The twenty-first century medium has a whole new shtick. Gone are
the darkened, moody parlors and spooky séances of yesteryear;

today, the realm of the medium generally consists of a well-lit stage, with an audience of sometimes hundreds of sitters, and with television cameras ready to capture every magical moment for viewers everywhere. Many psychics in this contemporary realm are vying for validity—not to mention, fame and fortune—but none has gotten more attention—good and bad—than medium John Edward.

With a kind of boyish earnestness, he serves as a two-way communication device: an approachable receptor from those who wish to deliver messages from beyond, and a charming, down-to-earth beacon of hope for those on this side who want to believe. For skeptics, however, he is seen as one of the most cunning, calculating, and heartless exploiters who ever lived . . . but we'll come back to that.

Edward's accuracy at any given sitting can be as much "miss" as it is "hit," but scores of followers remain devout, and this has much to do with his "regular Joe" delivery of messages from the dearly departed. In a manner that is as soft and mellow as it is intense, questions fly from him like machine-gun fire, until he finally makes a connection between beyond and bereaved. Self-effacing and admittedly skeptical himself, Edward provokes straightforward response— you either strongly believe him or you don't. As is the case with most of the psychics profiled in this book, a case—a strong case— can be made for both sides.

John Edward was born John MaGee Jr. in 1970, the only child of John MaGee, a police officer, and Perinda, in Glen Cove, Long Island. His parents' marriage was not a successful one, and his father split when Edward was in the sixth grade, leaving Perinda to raise her son on her own.

Such as is the case with most psychics, Edward's abilities began to surface in childhood. When he was only three years old, he reports remembering being able to leave his own body and "float" over to the homes of relatives. Proof of this came in him having tidbits of knowledge about members of his extended family and about his mother's childhood that had never been told to him.

Skeptics argue that these memories of Edward's were probably more influenced than actually real. His mother, to whom he was (and even in death remains) deeply devoted, was utterly fascinated by the supernatural when he was growing up. Perinda invited psychics to the house all the time, hosting séances and the like.

At one of these sittings, in 1985, Edward made the acquaintance of psychic Lydia Clar. By simply twirling his high school ring in her fingers, she told the fifteen-year-old John that he definitely had "the gift."

As John soon learned, "the gift" could be a very fun thing, and he used it often, informally, to read tarot cards and give palm readings. But sadly, he also quickly learned that "the gift" could be as much a curse as it was a blessing. When John was sixteen, he had a vision of his uncle's death that unfortunately came to pass. This caused Edward to feel a lot of frustration with his talent, because what good was it if he couldn't use it to help? Why should he be able to see things he had no control over?

Just a year and a half later, he felt himself let down again: Perinda was diagnosed with terminal cancer in 1989 and given only a few months to live. For some reason, John had not been able to predict this, and he was angry about it, that if it had been caught sooner, perhaps she would have been saved.

Skeptics say he couldn't predict his own mother's death because he is a fake and a phony; Edward says that although he hadn't realized it at the time, the reason he didn't see Perinda's death was that in the case of a relationship as strong and tight as mother and son, the emotions get in the way and cloud interpretation. Edward explained in an interview with Larry King that "when you're working with somebody that you don't know, you can be completely objective. And you can kind of just say, you know, 'Here you go, this is what I'm seeing, hearing, and feeling.' As soon as you start getting information that you can identify and know, then you have to stop and say, 'Well, I know that.' You know, so you can't be as objective and become subjective." This is the reason why, even all these years after her death, he communicates with his mother only through other mediums.

Psychic ability notwithstanding, Edward hadn't ever planned to make a living helping others communicate with the dead. After graduating from high school, he attended college and earned a degree in health care administration and public administration. For several years, he worked in a hospital as a phlebotomist—joking to Larry King that he was a "vampire. . . . I was the person you did not want to see . . . because I was going to be sticking you with needles, drawing your blood."

In 1992, Edward started taking dance lessons at Arthur Murray, thinking he might put a passion for ballroom dancing to financial use and become an instructor. The ballroom dance instructor plan didn't prove to be long term, but there was something in his lessons he took away with him for life: It was here where he met his wife, Sandra, who was his teacher and whom he married in 1995.

Throughout the 1990s, Edward continued his health administration work and dancing, but he never let go of his psychic universe, continuing to give readings in his spare time.

In 1999, Edward published his first book, *One Last Time*, about his life as a medium. It became a huge best seller and led to him landing his nationally syndicated television show *Crossing Over*, which hit the airwaves in July 2000. In this forum, he soon garnered the attention of the world, while he released subsequent best sellers.

It was really his TV show that opened the doors for skeptics' attacks. Many who had gone to tapings were surprised to see how often Edward missed the mark on his line of questioning. Others were suspicious of being eavesdropped on and/or recorded while waiting for the taping of the show to begin. Still others noticed after the fact, watching the episode in which they may have been featured, that the video had been edited and spliced together strategically to misrepresent what had actually happened—making the audience member nod or agree to something at which he or she distinctly remembers outwardly disagreeing with, and the like.

Such misinterpretations as these have fueled John Edward skeptics, especially magician James Randi, who is quite possibly the most outspoken opponent of psychics in the spotlight today—just think of him as the Harry Houdini of the modern world. Randi believes that Edward is little more than a master manipulator who gets his information not through special powers, but through a process called "cold reading." In cold reading, the questioner literally reads his subject cold, without knowing anything about him or her, whether from past experience or spirits spinning about. The cold reader shoots out tons of statements at once, frenetically whirling information around in an effort to confuse the questioner into believing that the information has not come from the questioner, but from someplace else. Edward's method of getting his facts reeks of similarity to this, which is one of the main things that makes him so controversial.

The most controversial maneuver Edward has made to date, however, which further spread the rift between skeptics and supporters, followed the tragic events of September 11, 2001. During this painful, vulnerable time, Edward planned to do a series of shows in which he would communicate with the victims and relay messages to their freshly grieving families. Plans were released October 25, barely six weeks after the event. Opposition and outrage forced the producers' hands and the shows were not broadcast; however, Edward still gave the sittings. When the wife of a firefighter who had perished in the Towers thanked Edward for giving her closure, he told *People Weekly*, "That's all I need to hear. Everyone else can bite me."

It's true that Edward doesn't let his critics get him down. He refuses to feed them with incessant denials and constant proof that he is legit. He flatly told *People Weekly* in another interview that "If you want to say I'm a fake, great, I'm not gonna defend it. It's a waste of time. The things that people say just don't make sense if they consistently watch."

What's interesting about the voices and messages that Edward brings through is that they are light and uplifting, usually infusing those to whom he relates them with a sense of calm, serenity, peace, and closure. Unlike folks like Ruth Montgomery (see page 175) and

Edgar Cayce (see page 61), among others, the souls that speak through Edward do not bring messages of apocalypse, world destruction, and doom. "Their message," he says, "is 'We're still around, we-love you.'"

Might the seeming altruistic John Edward someday give up the glamorous show-biz circuit and, like Elizabeth Joyce (see page 157) and other psychics, work with the police to help solve crimes? "I would not," the ever self-effacing Edward told Larry King. "I misinterpret all the time, so I would not want the responsibility."

So for now, Edward plans to continue his public work (though (*Crossing Over* ceased production) as well as to author more books about his psychic experiences. He still continues to see folks in his Huntington, Long Island, office for about $750 a pop—with a waiting list that's more than three years long. A TV drama is also in the works.

In a psychic career that's been a kind of back-and-forth between "why me" and "thank(ing) God me," the bottom line for Edward's appreciation for his actual—or perceived—gift, and why he does what he does, is best summed up in his own words, "I love the ability to be able to reunite people. . . . It's very, very rewarding, and it's a gift. That, to me, is—that completion of the circle is the gift."

Maria Esperanza
Mystic, Seer
(1928–)

I have also been able to see the transfiguration which happens to her when some gold spray seems to cover her hands and face and her body. It is a little film of gold spray. Also, the phenomenon of levitation has been taking place. I have testimony from many people about the transfiguration which takes place in her, the phenomenon of stigmata which takes place on Good Friday.

—Monsignor Pio Bello, who approved the apparition of Mary at Finca Betania

Born on November 22, the Feast Day of Saint Cecelia, in 1928, Maria Esperanza was raised in the small village of San Rafeal, which is in Barrancas, Monagas, Venezuela.

Even before Maria was born, her life was on a path of supreme influence by the Blessed Virgin. Maria's mother desperately wanted a daughter and prayed to Mary incessantly to bless her with one. Soon, the elder Esperanza was pregnant, and she continued her prayers. The birth was a painful and dangerous one, and throughout, Maria's mother continued to pray. At last, her prayers were answered. She named her brand new daughter "Maria," in honor of Mary.

Ever since she was a very young girl, Maria was religious. She was even known to dress her dolls up like priests and nuns. At age five, she had her first vision. St. Therese of Liseux, "the Little Flower," appeared to the child, rising from the banks of the Orinoco River. Therese presented Maria with a red rose, and disappeared again.

When Maria told her mother about what had happened, and gave her the rose, her mother saw that her daughter was indeed special and believed the passing of the rose to be a symbolic message from God: Therese had "passed the torch," in this case, the flower, to the girl to continue the work that she had started during her own short tenure on Earth. In time, every miracle Maria performed was centered in some way around roses. Though she nearly didn't live to fulfill her mission.

Maria was always a sickly child and adult, and she nearly died several times due to these illnesses.

At age twelve, Maria had a vision of the Virgin. At the time, she was "dying" of bronchial pneumonia. The Lady told Maria exactly what medicine she was to take to get better, and following the heavenly instruction, she was soon cured.

At age twenty-two, once again knocking at death's door, so sick that she was even paralyzed, she had another vision. This time, Jesus appeared to her and named her cure. Following this instruction, once again she was saved.

After that, her life's mission, to her, became abundantly clear. She wholeheartedly decided to follow in the footsteps of St. Therese and joined a convent of Franciscan nuns in Merida shortly after Jesus appeared to her.

It wouldn't be her last vision, however. Her life would again be altered by another heavenly vision—although this time, she wasn't sick.

On October 3, 1954, St. Therese appeared to Maria again. She again tossed the young nun a rose, but this time, when Maria looked at her fist to see the gift the saint brought her, she watched as the rose turned to blood. It was her first experience with the stigmata she would have throughout her life.

Therese told her to leave the convent. She had a destiny to fulfill, doing God's work, but this was not the way. In fact, her real mission was to travel the world and then to settle down, marry, and have many children.

What Therese had not told the young woman, however, was when she was to begin this new mission and where she was supposed to head first, so she remained basically inert at the convent, awaiting further instruction.

Jesus appeared to her this time and told her to travel, but to be sure to go to Rome. There, Maria felt the answers would come.

After seeing much of the world and starting to make a name for herself as a holy person and healer, Maria ended up in Rome. There, she met Geo Bianchini Giani. They were married in 1956 at the Chapel of the Immaculate Conception in St. Peter's Basillica. No one had ever been granted permission to marry there during Advent, but

Pope Pius XII had already heard of Maria and her exceptional works, so he personally granted permission for the Advent nuptials.

Where did the newlyweds go from there? After some more traveling, meeting people and performing miracles, Maria and her husband decided to settle in her native Venezuela. And thus occurred another passing of the torch.

Padre Pio, a priest she had met in her travels who was also regarded as a holy person, appeared to Maria on September 23, 1968. "Esperanza, I have come to say good-bye," he told her. "My time has come. It is your turn." Her husband reported that Maria's face was temporarily transfigured into that of the Italian priest. If he had had any doubt about his wife's special powers, this essentially wiped them all away. Well, that, and the news that Padre Pio had passed away; he was reported dead the next morning.

During her acquaintance with Padre Pio, he told her of a tract of land that was to become holy, and Maria and her husband spent a considerable number of years—1957 to 1974, in fact—trying to locate it. They finally found it in March 1974, half an hour outside of Caracas. The land was called Betania, and according to Geo, it corresponded perfectly with the visions his wife had been having of the spot.

In February 1976, Maria had another vision of the Virgin Mary, who appeared to Maria at Betania, to tell her that she had, in fact, found just the right spot. Mary would appear to Maria several more times in the coming years at Betania.

On March 25, 1984, seven apparitions were witnessed in the spot, and not just by Maria: 108 others also confirmed the appearances. In the months that followed, thousands more witnessed the apparition. To this day, Maria reports she sometimes receives more than one message per day from the Blessed Mother.

During her years back in Venezuela, Maria fulfilled the other part of the destiny she was told was hers. She became the mother of seven children; currently, she is also a grandmother to nineteen grandchildren.

Over the course of the years, Maria has been reported performing many miracles. Among her many "tricks," she has been able to make the Eucharist materialize in her mouth. She is a bilocater—meaning, she can be in more than one place at a time. She is also reported to exude a fragrance of flowers. A mystic and visionary, she is also a healer and has also been known to levitate. And then there's the stigmata that surfaces every Good Friday, without fail.

Perhaps the oddest thing associated with Maria Esperanza is that a rose has sprouted from her chest sixteen times. This has even been recorded on film, but she has said this footage is not to be released until her death.

Among the prophecies she's made are ones similar to the messages from the Fatima Seers (see page 103). Among these, Mary has told her about the global war and disease that will occur if humans don't change their ways and start praying to Mary.

Maria has met with, been accepted by, and is even supported by religious leaders the world over. In February 1998, she had a private audience with Pope John Paul II.

Of the miracle of Finca Betania, Monsignor Pio Bello Ricardo says that "by and large, apparitions have protagonists. In Finca Betania, nearly two thousand people have seen the apparitions. However, there is a main protagonist, she is Maria Esperanza Medrano de Bianchini . . . she was the first to see the apparitions . . . she saw the apparitions on numerous occasions before 1984 when the apparitions started to be seen by those two thousand people . . . [she] had received messages regarding a Holy Land where Our Lady would appear . . . [she] has seen the apparitions in Finca Betania many times."

This famed apparition was officially approved by the Catholic Church in 1987.

In 1991, a very strange phenomenon occurred. During a mass attended by Maria, the Host that a bishop was consecrating actually bled. "I had a scientific investigation conducted, and this was done by a laboratory that is totally trustworthy," reported the bishop. "They proved definitely that the substance that leaked from the Host was human blood."

By 1993, a local doctor, Vinicio Paz, estimated that Maria Esperanza had healed close to 1,000 people from various ailments—everything from cancer, to paralysis, to liver disorders, and more. And, to date, more than 10,000 people have witnessed the Virgin at Betania.

Maria has continued to travel extensively, as an ambassador of Mary and of her messages. That is, until 2002. She received word that the pope was ill and suffering a great deal, so she prayed that his pain would be transferred to her so he could continue his work. At the time of this writing, her condition, while she is still alive, cannot be confirmed.

Something like pain will not stand in Esperanza's way, however. As she still professes, "A great moment is approaching. A great day of light."

SISTER LUCY, CORBIS

The Fatima Seers

Prophecy

Lucia "Sister Lucy" dos Santos (1907–)
Francisco Marto (1908–1919)
Jacinta Marto (1910–1920)

Oh my Jesus, it is for love of You, for the conversion of sinners, and in reparation for the sins committed against the Immaculate Heart of Mary!

—Jacinta Marto

A psychic, as we have learned, is a person with extraordinary vision and ability, a person more in tune to realms other than the physical three dimensions we experience in our ordinary world. It is for this reason that the three little seers of Fatima fit snuggly into the category.

In a nutshell, for those not familiar with the story, the Virgin Mary appeared before these three children in 1917 and gave them messages intended to save the world from destruction, that the world would only be spared if humanity complied with the conditions in the messages. The three children were given three secrets, intended to be revealed at different times, for just this purpose.

Before Mary appeared, an angel came to the children to warn them so they would not be alarmed. This happened the year before the visits, and it has been supposed that the visiting angel was none other than Michael the Archangel, who essentially had come to teach the all-but-illiterate children how to pray so they would be prepared to receive the Lady.

Mary appeared a total of six times to these three children in Fatima, Portugal, between May 13 and October 13, 1917. Only one of the three survived to adulthood, and she is still alive—though well over ninety years old.

The Children

At the core of the visions of Fatima are the children themselves, so it's important to have a background of who they were before getting into the actual visions and their supposed meanings.

Lucia. The oldest of the three children, Lucia dos Santos was born on March 22, 1907, into a poor family in Portugal.

There wasn't much time for goofing off in the ten year old's life when Mary appeared to the children. Her father, Manuel, had essentially abandoned the family to take up with his "mistress," lady booze. Lucia's mother, Maria Rosa, was overstretched trying to provide for her family, and overworked making sure there was food on the table and clothes on their backs.

When Lucia first reported the visions to her parents, Manuel, who was likely drunk at the time, laughed the admission off and blamed it on "a child's imagination"; her mother had no time for such nonsense as imagination, however, and her disbelief turned to anger when the child would not admit to what seemed, even to the religious Sunday school teacher, an obvious lie. What could be worse would be to entertain the possibility of mental illness, and how, on top of the mother's already overburdened existence, how was she going to deal with an insane child?

The only one of the three Fatima Seers who made it to adulthood, Lucia left home at age fourteen to become a nun. After dedicated study, she entered the Convent of the Sisters of Saint Dorothy in 1925.

And Lucia continued to have visions. In 1925, Mary appeared to her with the baby Jesus in her arms and both spoke to her, reminding her of the message of Fatima. In 1927, Lucia was at last given permission to reveal the first "two secrets" to the world. (The secrets are discussed later in this chapter.) And in 1938, all she saw in terms of a vision was a streak across the sky. Lucia interpreted that as the start of World War II—although most everyone else who saw it that night interpreted it as the aurora borealis.

Francisco. The sixth child of Manuel Pedro Marto and Olimpia de Jesus dos Santos, Francisco spent most of his time hanging around with his sister, Jacinta, and their cousin, Lucia.

He took Sunday school, taught by his aunt, Lucia's mother, and his catechism got him interested in devoting his life to God. After the angel appeared to him, his sister, and cousin, he was totally transformed from a boy with an unusual interest in God to servant of the Lord. He was known to have started praying at the drop of a hat; in fact, he spent most of his time praying and looking forward to going to heaven. "How beautiful God is, how beautiful!" he proclaimed. "But He is sad because of the sins of men. I want to console Him, I want to suffer for the love of Him." After the visions at Fatima,

Francisco went to penance all the time in preparation for his own death and entrance to heaven. In October 1918, he contracted the Spanish flu and died about six months later, on April 4, 1919.

Francisco was beatified for sainthood by the pope on May 13, 2000.

Jacinta. Jacinta Marto became the seventh child in the large Marto clan when she was born March 11, 1910. She spent all of her time with her brother, Francisco, and cousin, Lucia, and was also taught catechism by her aunt, cousin Lucia's mother.

When she was still a very young girl, she was put to work as a shepherd with her brother and Lucia. Jacinta is reported to have been a "lively, playful child"; after the visits, she became more solemn and loving and devoted her life to prayer. "I love our Lord so much!" she said. "At times, I seem to have a fire in my heart, but it does not burn me."

Jacinta could not get enough of the stories about the life and pain and Passion of Christ. The truth be known, the child was perhaps getting a little "weird" and began to be ostracized by children she once called playmates. It didn't matter to her; she knew she was not long for this world, on her way to heaven, and she remained devout, praying and even fasting.

In 1918, she, like brother Francisco, came down with the Spanish flu and was sick for a very long time. Eventually, when doctors in her small town could do nothing more for her, she was moved to a hospital far away from home in Lisbon, where she died, alone, but "in the company of God," on February 20, 1920.

Along with Francisco, she was beatified for sainthood by the pope on May 13, 2000.

The Visits

Mary appeared to the children several times between May and October 1917, and these visits became the stuff of Catholic legend.

During Mary's first visit, on May 13, 1917, the children all saw a bright blue flash of light dart across the sky. Then, a glowing ball appeared, and inside the ball was a beautiful woman who spoke to them. While all the children could see her, Francisco could not hear her, though his sister and cousin could and told him everything the Lady said. This visit was more a greeting than anything else; Mary told the children that she would return five more times with important information.

By June 13, word had spread throughout the small village that Mary had appeared to the children and was going to appear again, so, this time, when the children went back to the spot, interested and curious fellow villagers tagged along.

When the children were settled into their spot, the Sun dimmed, and Mary appeared. This time, Mary told the children they needed to learn to read and write. She also revealed that Jacinta and Francisco would soon be called back to heaven.

On July 13, more crowds amassed and followed the children to the site. On this day, the first of the three secrets was revealed to the children: the vision of hell and what Mary needed humanity to do to avoid going there.

On August 13, the children were tricked and kidnapped before they could get to the spot where their vision would appear. They were finally able to escape and made their way to the spot, a wee bit late, on August 19. The Virgin knew they would be there and appeared for them. This time, she gifted them with fragrant branches that, when brought home to their parents, even caused Lucia's mother to start to believe.

On September 13, there were thousands who appeared this time to see the vision, which lasted only seconds. The message was to pray the rosary to end the war.

On October 13, 1917, the date of the last vision, there was either a true vision of heaven or an unexplainable mass group hallucination occurred. This time, more than 70,000 spectators had gathered but couldn't in their wildest dreams imagine what they were about to see. Documented as the "Miracle of the Sun," in this vision, the Sun was reported to dance about the sky, threatening to descend on the earth, but pulling away before its proximity became a real threat. While the spectacle was going on, Mary delivered to the children news of the end of the war and the third of the mysterious "secrets."

The Secrets

While the children were given a view of what was to be known as the three secrets of Fatima, it wasn't until 1925 that Mary gave permission, to Lucia, to reveal the secrets. Lucia was told she could reveal the "third secret" either before 1960 or after her own death, whichever came first.

First secret. The children were given a horrifying vision of hell. It was told to them by Mary that this is where humanity was headed before too long if people did not start to take things seriously.

Second secret. Mary told the children that World War I was going to end very shortly and that the end could be expedited with prayers, but she warned that World War II was inevitable. She said that Russia needed to be consecrated to her or that more destruction would occur, and there was nothing that could be done about it unless these instructions were followed.

The first two secrets were revealed in the 1930s; the last would not be revealed for nearly seventy years.

Third secret. In May 2000, Pope John Paul II authorized Cardinal Angelo Sodano to reveal the third secret before an audience of 600,000 spectators who had gathered to hear the message. The cardinal read, "He makes his way toward the cross amid the corpses of those who were martyred. He, too, falls to the ground, apparently under a burst of gunfire."

Essentially, the third part of the secret, as explained by the Church, was that the pope was going to be shot, which may explain why so many popes before John Paul II who had been privy to the information kept it under wraps. What is dubious about the admission, however, is that it took until 2000 for the secret to be revealed, when it was commanded to be revealved nearly 40 years prior. If the prediction was in fact the assassination attempt, and that happened in 1981, why the nearly twenty-year lag?

Some believe the secret is more expansive and that the shooting of the pope is only part of it. Some are still waiting for the rest of the secret to be revealed, believing that what it really divulges is the date of the much-feared Judgment Day.

Sonya Fitzpatrick
Animal Communicator
(1940–)

Words cannot do her arrival justice to the magic that came with her. I could feel her presence was something special. She's for real. I know it with every fiber that makes me alive. It's absolutely wonderful.

—Robin Taylor Corbridge, pet owner
who appeared on Animal Planet's
The Pet Psychic

What do models do when they mature past their youth and need to settle into another career? If they have suppressed psychic talents, like famed animal communicator and pet psychic Sonya Fitzpatrick, they may eventually find themselves calling on those lost talents again. Sonya's charismatic, infectious charm, lively sense of humor, and undeniable warmth comes right off her. And her British accent, sounding much like Julie Andrews in *Mary Poppins* or *The Sound of Music*, endears people to her. You just *want* to

COURTESY OF SONYA FITZPATRICK

trust her because she really seems able to tell you what your beloved pets are saying.

Now whether she really does pull it off comes under much debate; as is the case with any psychic, the believability element has to be factored in. It's undeniable that her utter compassion for animals is glowingly apparent. She clearly puts animals, and, subsequently, their owners, at ease. Does she really know what the animals are saying? Is she a true-to-life Doctor Dolittle? That's up to the individual.

Certainly, and with little surprise, James Randi doesn't buy into her brand of animal telepathy. "She's essentially playing a game of twenty questions with the [pet owner]," he says. "People who believe in what she does are naïve." That line of thinking doesn't faze Fitzpatrick, however. She has never been formally tested and doesn't "feel that it's necessary." She doesn't feel that she has "to prove anything to anybody scientifically."

Many psychic experiences are shaped in childhood. This holds especially true when it comes to Fitzpatrick, who grew up surrounded by animals. Born in the English countryside in 1940 into a rural family, Sonya was born with a hearing impairment that isolated her in many ways from the human world, but she never turned a deaf ear to animals. "I talked to animals before people," she told *Newsweek*. "I had a hearing loss, so I didn't talk until I was four. My mother likes to say I haven't stopped since."

Sonya has said that when she was a child, "talking to animals was as natural as breathing" and she naturally assumed everyone could do it. "The animals could always hear me and I thought everybody could do what I was doing."

One of the most significant early relationships she had with an animal was with her terrier, Judy. Essentially her best friend as a child, Judy and Sonya spent all their time together. But, as dogs do, Judy eventually got old and sick. Around the end, Sonya says she could feel every ache and pain Judy was feeling holding the little dog in her arms.

But she eventually got over that loss. Her most significant lesson in human-animal relations was yet to happen.

The most traumatic experience Sonya had with animals in her childhood occurred with a trio of geese she had befriended, practically from the time of their hatching. Anyone who's ever had animals knows the bond one can forge with them, especially when one raises them from birth. Most animal lovers never go through the hardest thing Sonya ever had to endure. Almost too gruesome to report, when the geese were nine months old, they were slaughtered, stuffed, and served up for Christmas dinner—a purpose that had always been in store for them but one that was inconceivable for Sonya.

From that point on, Sonya became a vegetarian. But, more significant yet, the shock and the horror of that slaughter and forced feast caused her to shut out the voices of the animals completely. And she did so for quite a few years to come.

When Sonya was seventeen, she became a fashion model. She became an international success, appearing in fashion magazines—even on covers—throughout the world, as well as on television. In

1991, she moved from London to the United States. Today, she still calls America "home," living in Texas with her four cats and seven dogs.

Her plan for making a living in the States was to start an etiquette business, which she did, with great success.

Nearly forty years had gone by since she heard the "voices" of animals when, in 1994, Sonya had a spiritual revelation. St. Francis of Assisi appeared to her and told her it was time to lift the embargo on her blocking out the "voices" of the animals. He told her that the animals needed her and that it was time to begin a third career: this time as a pet psychic. "He told me I would be doing God's work," she told *People Weekly*. So Sonya opened the lines of communication again, first with her own pets and then with the pets of others.

By 1997, she had worked with so many animals, she published a book about her experiences, *What the Animals Tell Me*. That book became a best seller, and from that point, she had become an internationally known pet psychic and began to make hundreds of appearances throughout the world.

On June 3, 2002, she launched her television show *The Pet Psychic*, on Animal Planet. The response was phenomenal and it has been one of their top-rated one-hour shows since its debut.

Today, the international animal communicator psychic continues to act as a consultant to all animals—from the most primitive-seeming fish and reptilian species to the highest mammals—and has become a conduit of communication between animals and their humans. She helps humans to understand their pets' feelings and thoughts, along the lines of "I like when you do this" and "I didn't like the time when you did this." In addition to solving domestic disputes, she has also aided in the rescue of lost or abandoned pets and helped sick animals communicate ailments to their owners. Says Sonya, "Anything that has a consciousness can understand and they get pictures and they talk in the same way a dog or cat would."

What are some of the messages Sonya has been able to convey from pet to human?

- She dragged the awful truth from a horse about his past: Before his current human took him in, he was about to be sent off to become horsemeat, and while he trusted his current human, this was a possibility that still nagged at him.

- She got a skittish dog rescued from a shelter to admit that she was afraid of going back to the shelter and that she really likes to wear a bandanna around her neck.

- She made a bird feel comfortable about confessing that he terrorized the family dog because he was jealous of all the attention the dog got from *his* humans and that he'd like his "mommy" to go back to playing the piano for him.

- She got an alligator to admit he was annoyed with his human for constantly feeding him chicken instead of the red meat that he preferred.

There are hundreds more stories like these. Of course, the only way to know for sure is to ask the pet's "parents" if what Sonya said was correct. And that's why so many believe her. When asked, the "parents" can always verify that Sonya is correct.

Also a pet medium, Sonya speaks with dead animals as well. "There are world upon worlds when we pass over," she says. "We don't die, we go on to the spiritual realm, we go home. [It is] the same with animals. . . . The consciousness goes on. The spirit travels on."

Her latest book, *Cat Talk: The Secrets of Communicating with Your Cat* (2003), was received with much anticipation and is also doing very well.

The highly passionate animal advocate participates in countless programs to protect and save animals, including her own nonprofit Gift of Animal Life Sanctuary. Sonya is currently moving into making her new super premium pet food line, Sonya Fitzpatrick's Omega Natural Pet Foods, which was developed by Sonya and a renowned animal nutritionist for dogs and cats.

For Sonya, the most rewarding aspect of her work is her ability to communicate one-to-one with animals and their human companions. Because of her gift, Sonya is able to help pet parents to better understand their beloved pets, and for animals to better understand their human companions.

Leslie Flint

Independent Direct Voice Medium

(1911–1994)

*I think I can safely say I am the most talented
medium this country has ever produced and, I will
add, the medium most willing to be tested whenever I
have felt truth would be served by submitting to
conditions imposed on me by those I have believed to
be genuine researchers. I have been boxed up, tied up,
sealed up, gagged, bound and held and still the voices
have to come to speak their message of life eternal.*

—Leslie Flint

Every psychic has a gimmick, a personal paranormal claim to fame. British-born Leslie Flint's claim was to externally channel those passed—and especially, well, the *famous*. Among those who reportedly spoke through Flint were Rudolph Valentino, Arthur Conan Doyle, Leslie Howard, Queen Victoria, Sir Winston Churchill, Maurice Chevalier, Mahatma Gandhi, and Charlotte Brontë, as well as many others.

In a career that spanned more than fifty years, the uncanny articulation of the voices that resonated through his external "voice box" remain an enigma of science, technology, and spirituality. And, unlike many psychics, even into his old age Flint proclaimed that he performed his work for humanitarian purposes first and foremost, that money and fame never mattered to him. When one takes a look at his life and career, one has no choice but to believe that, whether what he claimed and showed he was able to do is believed or not.

Born in 1911 in one of the most impoverished sections of London, Flint was not expected. His mother and father were married only after his birth. The marriage was a disaster, and neither of his parents seemed interested in sticking around to raise their son. Flint's father escaped his misery in a haze of excessive drinking and gambling, and then finally by enlisting in the army in 1914. Whether he survived the war or not is not known; Flint never heard from him again.

Extricated from the nuptial noose, Flint's mother soon began to lead the colorful life a young, unhappily married woman who finds herself suddenly single, and full of opportunity and sex appeal might opt to lead. Within a couple of years, however, she eloped, leaving her old life behind, including her young son. Flint went to live with his grandmother in yet another impoverished section of London called St. Albans. From one wrong side of the tracks to another, the move to grandma's was lateral at best, but at least in this situation he had a less indifferent caregiver.

From a young age, Flint had begun hearing voices he couldn't identify—and that no one else seemed to hear—but his first significant encounter with the paranormal was when he was seven years old. News came that the husband of Flint's aunt Nell, his uncle Alf, whom he had never met, had been killed in the war. Shortly thereafter, Flint watched as a soldier tugged at his aunt's sleeve one day when she was working in the kitchen. The aunt didn't acknowledge the man, who soon vanished. Flint realized only he could see him. When he was later shown a photo of his dead uncle, he told his aunt and grandmother about the vision he had in the kitchen. This earned him a smack in the head, and it became an early lesson in keeping those things he saw to himself.

Never a great student, Flint dropped out of school at age thirteen. Thereafter, he kept himself occupied with various odd jobs,

which ranged from being a gardener and groundskeeper of a cemetery, to movie projectionist, to tailor, to ballroom dance instructor,
the last of which he truly felt would be his career. Even as a teenager,
though he decided still to keep quiet about his ability, he remained
curious about the visions he continued to have and eventually
attended a meeting for the local Theosophical Society. This sparked
him into thinking more about spiritualism and communication with
the dead. Most of what was discussed at the meeting was well
beyond Flint's comprehension, however, so he set out to find more
casual forums.

At seventeen, Flint attended his first séance. The medium told
Flint that an older man who had passed was looking out for him,
and she described, to a T, a former teacher of Flint's, who had taken
a quasi-paternal interest in him while Flint was still in school. Flint
was intrigued, but the more meetings of this kind he attended, the
less patience he had for most so-called mediums, many of which he
perceived as merely taking wild stabs in the dark and making things
up, trying to get a hit, and exploiting their subjects in the process.

Despite his frustration with all the chicanery, Flint didn't lose
his interest in spiritualism and soon began getting messages directed
to him encouraging him to become a medium himself. Most notable
at this time was a spirit who came through time and again, whom
Flint would recognize as "someone dressed as an Arab." Torn
between being intrigued by the notion that he had the ability to
communicate with the dead and his anger with those who also
claimed the same ability, whom he perceived as frauds, Flint
remained skeptical.

One day, Flint received a letter from a woman in Munich, who
said she was writing to him to communicate a message from the
deceased Rudolph Valentino. In life, Valentino had had a known
interest in spiritualism. Apparently, Valentino had come through in
her particular circle, requesting that she get in touch with Flint, and
even providing her with Flint's home address. From beyond the
grave, Valentino had told her that Flint was a powerful medium who
was letting his powers go to waste and that the time had come for

him to start using them. When Flint read that the request was coming from Valentino, he was stunned but not amazed. At this point, he made the connection between his guide being "someone dressed as an Arab" and the famed actor who had tragically passed a few years prior and whose most famous film role was that of *The Sheik*, a character dressed as an Arab.

Around this time, Flint met Edith Mundin, a member of a local spiritualist church, and she persuaded him to join her circle. Impressed by his talent, Edith convinced Leslie, finally, to use his gift by acting as medium at various private sittings, which he conducted with great success. At age twenty-four, Flint gave his first public demonstration and became an immediate hit with sitters and skeptics alike.

Sitters believed they had finally found a genuine connection to the other side; skeptics were excited to have a hot new target to sniff out, whom they immediately deemed a money-grubbing fraud. They were wrong about the money part at the very least. "There was no money made. I didn't get any fees," Flint explains in his autobiography. "We did it because we wanted to help comfort and uplift mankind." That Flint was a "fraud" was something skeptics bent over backward to try and prove until his death—and are still grappling with nearly ten years hence—though most who didn't believe have eventually found themselves converted.

In Flint's heyday, his séances could draw as many as 2,000 anxious sitters at a time. He, however, preferred the confines of a sitting room or parlor—with an intimate group of people used to meditating with one another—to a hall full of gawking, anonymous strangers. Especially later in life, he was notorious in the psychic world for publicly denouncing mediums who "made a spectacle" of the gift by playing to large audiences and writing countless books. In an interview with the Noah's Ark Society shortly before his death, he said that those who looked at this way of life as a way to get rich were "like pop stars. I think they're letting the movement down."

Flint is unique in the medium milieu as he is one of a few psychics who communicated messages externally; it was the spirit's "own voice" that sitters heard—and not directly from Flint. In a typical Flint séance, Flint and the sitters would wait in a dark room for spirits to arrive. When they "spoke," they didn't use Flint's mouth. Instead, they communicated through an independent voice box, created by ectoplasm, situated outside of him. As Flint describes in his autobiography, "I have a rare gift known as the independent direct voice. I do not speak in trance, I need no trumpets or other paraphernalia. The voices of the dead speak directly to their friends or relatives and are located in space a little above my head and slightly to one side of me. They are objective voices which my sitters can recall." When they came through, people could actually recognize the sometimes muffled and other times quite clear voices of their loved ones.

Ectoplasm is known in the paranormal world as residue left by spirits, which enables them to materialize. Flint described ectoplasm and how he used it as a "life force. . . . During a séance, this substance, which is sometimes referred to as 'the power,' is drawn from the body and fashioned by spirits into a replica of the physical vocal organs which is known as the voice-box or sometimes the mask. The communicating spirit then concentrates his or her thoughts into this voice-box." Flint's brand of ectoplasm could only exist outside his body and in total darkness. If a light was turned on, the ectoplasm would rush back in to Flint and could cause him severe pain and even result in his death.

Skeptics speculated that because Flint was not "on" all the time and that because he worked in the dark, he was up to no good, pulling the wool over darkened eyes. For this, but more importantly because he seemed so accurate, Flint was scrupulously tested, which Flint supported for the sake of science. In some instances, he was made to conduct séances with his mouth filled with water; in others, his lips were plastered shut. The technology of the day wasn't sophisticated enough to explain the voices that way, yet still the voices came.

Skeptics only got satisfaction when Flint would not be able to pull voices through. They said that he choked, much to his annoyance. He explained that true psychic phenomena cannot be prompted, that "[y]ou have got to realize there's no guarantee that it will work or will happen."

The skeptics soon started to wear his patience thin. "When I first began to allow myself to be tested I was naive enough to believe that if the tests were successful the scientists and researchers who carried them out under their own conditions would proclaim to all the world the truth of life after death," he recounted in his autobiography. He believed incorrectly. What actually happened, in his account, was that instead of approaching Flint's gift with an open mind, the scientists, a la the skeptics, proposed every kind of theory they could think of to disprove him; some so outrageously unlikely that even with today's technology, these suppositions could not be supported. But even though they buzzed around him like mosquitoes, Flint never turned down any opportunity to endure what he deemed their "ridiculous testing"; as a result, he was able to wear many of them down, converting some skeptics into true believers.

Flint never had anything to hide and was not proprietary over the voices that spoke through him. He even permitted anyone who wanted to tape his sessions, and people did. So what did the voices say? Charlotte Brontë chatted about the purpose of creative people. Maurice Chevalier talked about his ambivalence to enter the spirit domain and the difficulty he faced with the transition. One of the most popular voices heard was that of Mickey, an eleven-year-old cockney boy who had been killed by a truck. Flint's number-one spirit guide, Mickey was probably much like Flint when he was a boy, a poor urchin and a bit rough around the edges.

For all the years Flint actively worked as a medium, he continued to be tested and slowly converted some of his critics. Through it all, his beloved Edith remained his main support system and his grounding guide through the mortal domain. When she died, he realized he was exhausted and decided to retire from public work. Flint never stopped believing that his life and work had meaning; if not, he concluded, "all the sitting in the dark is unimportant."

He continued to conduct private sittings, and especially looked forward to sitting with George Woods, whom he had been sitting with since 1946, and Betty Greene, who joined his circle in 1953. Especially in the sittings with these two, Flint reported receiving more information and notoriety than he had in his career. Greene and Woods devoted their lives to tracking, recording, preserving, and then distributing copies of the recorded voices that spoke through Flint until their deaths in 1975 and 1983, respectively.

Flint died on April 16, 1994. Shortly thereafter, friends of Flint wanted to make sure that Flint's legacy lived on in this realm, so the Leslie Flint Educational Trust (www.LeslieFlint.com) was officially established in 1997. The nonprofit organization continues to spread his message and prove his validity by providing tapes of Flint's sittings and educating others to believe Flint's own words that "death is not the end . . . the person they've known and loved still exists and at all times is able to come near them, and that one day they will meet again on the Other Side of life."

The Fox Sisters

Mediums, Clairvoyants

Margaretta, a.k.a. "Maggie" (c. 1840–1893)
Catherine a.k.a. "Kate" (c. 1842–1892)

It was the greatest sorrow of my life. I began the deception when I was too young to know right from wrong.

—Margaretta Fox, taken from her 1888 confession at the New York Academy of Music

What would you think if you found out that the modern spiritualism movement in America was sparked by the antics and

LIBRARY OF CONGRES

believed abilities of two young mischievous and "talented" young girls?

Whatever your personal reaction might be, the truth is what it is. On Friday night, March 31, 1848, in the middle of the night, two young girls, from their bedroom in Hydesville, New York, communicated with—or claim to have communicated with—the dead. Known familiarly as "The Hydesville Rappings," the incident, in time, led to the discovery of the remains of a man who had been murdered in the house. It also led to a pair of careers both famous and infamous; the sisters had about a million followers by 1855.

Devout Methodists and parents of six children, John and Margaret Fox moved into a house in Hydesville with their two youngest daughters, Catherine (Kate) and Margaretta (Maggie), in December 1847. They were elated about the move. They had gotten a good deal on the house because the previous owner was anxious to vacate. Apparently, strange noises were resonating in the night and the previous owners were creeped out. The Foxes had a great laugh at their good luck, as they were not superstitious folk and didn't believe in haunted houses. At least not yet.

For months, the house was quiet. But then, in March 1848, things started to happen. Maggie and Kate, about ten and seven years old, respectively, at first seemed scared by the unexplainable noises, which could include any combination of knocks, footsteps, or random vibrations. But instead of being frightened to death, they decided to take control of the situation. As their mother recounts in an affidavit she made and signed concerning the incidents, "On Friday night, March 31st, 1848, we concluded to go to bed early and not permit ourselves to be disturbed by the noises. . . . I knew it from all the other noises I had ever heard before. The children, who slept in the other bed in the room, heard the rapping, and tried to make similar sounds by snapping their fingers." Instead of being afraid, the girls took matters into their own hands—or at least seemed to.

It was Kate who first tried to communicate with the source of the rappings. She boldly asked the spirit to identify itself, using a code she developed. She told the visitor that when she asked a question and when it wanted to answer, one rap would mean "yes" while two meant "no."

Eventually, the girls came to call him "Mr. Splitfoot" and were able to ascertain that he was a thirty-one-year-old peddler named Charles Rosna, who had been murdered and buried in the house.

The commotion rocked the neighborhood. An initial investigation by police at the time uncovered little by way of proof; it wasn't until the summer that authorities were able to dig deep into the basement and turn up a skull fragment and hair. Still, it would take yet another fifty-six years, long after the little girls lived their lives and they themselves died, before a further investigation turned up a man's body, buried in the walls of the house.

Despite the conclusive proof that would come so much later, the revelation was soon bringing constant visitors to the house—friends, neighbors, and the press. A report by E. E. Lewis, "A Report of the Mysterious Noises Heard in the House of Mr. John D. Fox," became the first-ever spiritualist publication.

This article sparked a widespread medium mania. All of a sudden, people everywhere began professing their own supersensory powers and were conducting séances as often as dinner parties.

Because of all the commotion, John and Margaret sent their daughters to live with their older siblings. After this point, it's nearly impossible to ascertain what happened to the parents. Kate went to David, her brother, in Auburn, New York, and Maggie to nearby Rochester to live with their much-older sister Leah Fish. Mr. and Mrs. Fox felt the exposure to the spirits and to the crowds was harmful and they wanted to protect the young girls from the spirits. But while there was never any word of the parents again, the spirits continued to visit the girls, both at David's and at Leah's—and worse at Leah's, where Maggie, who would come to be regarded as the more powerful medium of the two, was staying.

Soon, both Kate and Maggie were both living with Leah and her teenaged daughter. Leah's husband had left her years before, so Leah was not exactly in the position to support three girls. So Leah exploited her sisters, first allowing people into her home to gawk at the young girls'—and especially Maggie's—talent. Leah even went so far as to arrange shows in public halls and collected a $1 admission from eager spectators. Even though it was Kate, and especially Maggie, who had the powers, Leah also called herself a medium and conducted séances. She wasn't stupid. She saw an easy route to revenue and jumped on it. Most reports confirm that Leah had no psychic powers at all; she was a pure fraud.

As they became more and more well known, the Fox sisters began to hold their own séances, which usually drew famous people—in both the physical and spiritual realm—but at times to disastrous ends. Maggie especially could not always bring voices through correctly. Once, when she allegedly pulled Ben Franklin through, his grammar was ridiculous, which made more than one person raise an eyebrow in doubt. Still a young kid, she didn't have the capacity, wherewithal, or capability for deceit (choose one) to explain that the voices didn't always come through as actual voices, that they sometimes came through as thoughts and energy. Still and all, many high-profile spiritualism enthusiasts attended Maggie's séances, including James Fennimore Cooper, Harriet Beecher Stowe, and William Cullen Bryant. The most notable attendee to Kate's séances was the recent widow of Abraham Lincoln, Mary Todd Lincoln, who wished to communicate with her dead husband.

Whatever the skeptics said, those interested in the psychic world embraced the children. P.T. Barnum saw their potential as an attraction and took them to New York City, and then throughout the country. One of their greatest supporters, Horace Greeley, at that time editor of the *New York Tribune*, even offered to house the girls and pay for their education. Leah, who was still their legal guardian at the time said this was okay for Kate, the lesser of the mediums, but there was still much money to be made on Maggie, so she kept this sister close at hand.

As is the case for many psychics, for as many followers as they had, the sisters also had their share of enemies and nonbelievers who did whatever they could to disprove and destroy the girls. This pack of rabid nonbelievers included a relative, Mrs. Norman Culver, who admitted that the girls had taught her to make the noises they had. "Catherine told me to warm my feet . . . she sometimes had to warm her feet three or four times in the course of an evening. . . . I have sometimes produced 150 raps in succession."

That admission set the skeptics all over the girls, who proposed that they performed their "tricks" by cracking their own joints and relying on ventriloquism. None of this, however, was ever proven, despite countless studies made on the sisters. That is, until 1850, when doctors in Buffalo explained the phenomenon as having to do with the children popping out their own knee joints. Still, they enjoyed a healthy and strong following.

It's amazing that for all the effort their parents made trying to give the girls a normal life, they would never be able to appreciate that kind of luxury. From the moment they realized their shared destinies, their lives began to take a downward spiral, and everything they did would be tainted by their "talent."

By the mid to late 1850s, Maggie embraced Catholicism, which would prove her spiritualist downfall later in life, but we'll get to that later. What it also meant, at least for the time being, was that she gave up being a medium. It simply did not conform to her new belief system.

Both sisters found love in their lives, but for each, it ended badly. Maggie faux-married famed aristocrat and Arctic explorer Elisha Kent Kane, whose family did not approve of the "marriage" because she was "below" him in social station. When he died in 1857, she inherited nothing, so she was forced to return to medium work. And then there was the drink.

Kate also started to become a raging alcoholic but, as she hadn't given up mediumship, she remained fairly successful at it. She left the States and went to England, where she met and married Henry Jencken in 1872. The couple had two sons, Ferdinand, who showed psychic promise, and another, who did not.

Tragically, Henry died of a stroke in 1885. Having nothing left for her in England, she returned to the States and picked up her old profession. She hadn't let go of her old habit: namely, booze, and got herself so consistently drunk that she had near-constant run-ins with the law. Her children were taken away from her when she was arrested in 1888. After that, there was not a lot left for her. She lived on booze and welfare.

In 1885, Maggie was called before a commission to prove her skills. She failed miserably. It was the last straw.

In 1888, at the New York Academy of Music, Maggie publicly admitted that she and her sisters were frauds, had always been frauds, and she denounced spiritualism. The desperate woman, whom no one would believe, even played out her tricks on stage. "My sister Katie was the first one to discover that by swishing her fingers she could produce a certain noise with the knuckles and joints, and that the same effect could be made with the toes," she said. "No one suspected us of any trick because we were such young children . . . all the neighbors thought there was something and they wanted to find out what it was. They were convinced someone had been murdered in the house."

Still, followers were not convinced that this was the truth. So she continued to dissect what they had done and how they had been paying for it all these years. "As far as spirits were concerned, neither my sister nor I thought about it," she said. "I have seen so much miserable deception that I am willing to assist in any way and to positively state that Spiritualism is a fraud of the worst description. I do so before my God, and my idea is to expose it . . . I trust that this statement, coming solemnly from me, the first and most successful in this deception, will break the force of the rapid growth of Spiritualism and prove that it is all a fraud, a hypocrisy and a delusion."

Even at the time it was going on, supporters of spiritualism believed Maggie made this "confession" because she was drunk and destitute and didn't really mean what she was saying. Also, they believed it was to spite her older sister/business manager, Leah, who had since married well and left them in a lurch. Especially after this, Leah cut herself off from her sisters and lived comfortably off the money they made for her, not to mention her remarriage to a successful businessman, until her death in 1890.

Kate publicly disagreed with Maggie's conclusion and continued to practice mediumship. By 1891, Maggie regretted what she had done and tried to take her statements back. It was too late. Maggie Fox had pulled a "Medea job" on spiritualism; she was the mother who murdered her young. And that was the end for them.

In any case, salvation was not to be found in either woman's lifetime. Kate died in July 1892; her body was discovered by her sons. Maggie held on only a few months more, herself dying due to drink in March 1893.

Many years after the sisters' deaths, a source leaked that Maggie may have been offered $1,500 by a reporter to denounce the Fox sisters' work. While it may not seem like a lot of money to sell out for by modern standards, at the time it was a pretty hefty chunk of change. It cannot be forgotten how destitute the women were at the point of Maggie's confession, and many believers stand fast that she only denounced spiritualism because she was desperate and because she had been put up to it.

Whatever the reason, the confession has not tarnished the Foxes in the eyes of true believers. The sisters continue to be remembered as the "mothers of the modern spiritualist movement."

G

Uri Geller

Telepath, Clairvoyant

(1946–)

Uri Geller's ability to perform amazing feats of mental wizardry is known the world over. . . . Uri is not a magician. He is using capabilities that we all have and can develop with exercise and practice.

—Dr. Edgar Mitchell, *Apollo 14* astronaut

In Hebrew, the name "Uri" translates into "hope and light"; in terms of getting the "tentative" to believe in the powers of ESP,

Uri Geller's name was certainly appropriate in the 1970s especially, when he astounded millions with abilities that had really not ever been seen before.

Widely known as the "father of mental bending," Geller made his television debut on November 23, 1973, when he appeared on a British program and telepathically bent spoons. That opened the floodgates: After the show was televised, people everywhere started experimenting with their own flatware, and they, too, learned they had a similar talent.

Geller reportedly could do more, however, than simply bend spoons. He could use his talent to bend anything made of metal, like keys, as well as stop and restart watches.

Naturally, Geller was scrupulously tested. The most grueling of these tests happened at the Stanford Research Institute. The results: He could not be proven a fraud. But that didn't stop the endless stream of tests. "Whatever I did was never enough," he said. "Whenever I finished one set of experiments, then another set of tests was wanted by another set of scientists. . . . It was hard for them to believe I was for real. I had to go through so many laborious tests." And still, he could not be shown up, no matter how many tests he was given.

A Hungarian-Austrian, Geller today lives in England. He was born in Tel Aviv, Israel, on December 20, 1946, to Margaret and Tibor Geller, his father a British soldier who fought in World War II.

Geller's parents divorced when Uri was young. His mother, whom he lived with, married Ladisalis Gero, and he and his mother moved to Cyprus, which was Gero's home. There, he learned English, but the environment he grew up in was less than luxurious. "I come from a very poor family and we struggled all my childhood," Geller has said.

His first paranormal experience happened when he was only an infant, but he claims to remember it. As the story goes, a bomb hit the side of the house where he and his parents lived, in England, when he was six months old. At that moment, a teddy bear kept in his crib, leapt from his side to cover his face and protect him from the debris about to land on him.

His second experience happened when he was playing in an abandoned garden he found behind a rusty iron fence when he was four years old. "The day before I had slid through a gap in the fence into the garden finding a rusty old rifle, it was real menacing looking," he says. "I took it out, and tried hitting it against the floor to see if there were any bullets in the barrel." It was empty.

The next day, he went back looking for another rifle, but there was none. Instead, he heard what sounded like kittens crying, and then there was a much larger sound. "[S]omething struck me," he said, and he was physically overpowered, knocked over by a beam of light. He scurried out of the garden right away, never to return.

Later that day, he ate his lunch, not having reported the occurrence in the garden to anyone. When he was through, and his mother cleared his place, she saw that the spoon he had been eating with had been bent. She essentially ignored the incident, chalking it off to the antics of a nervous child.

From then, he lived a relatively normal life, except that he became fully aware of his gifts and began making them more and more public. It was his gift of prophecy that he used at a cocktail party where Prime Minister Golda Meir was also in attendance. He impressed her with his gifts, and has since thanked her for launching him and his ability into the spotlight. After the party, during a radio interview about the future of Israel, Meir jokingly quipped, "Don't ask me, ask Uri Geller."

Enough people knew his name at the time, and if Meir was going to "take him seriously," then so were they.

In 1971, Geller met Andrija Puharich, who introduced him to former astronaut Edgar Mitchell, who helped research Uri's gift. Uri underwent a series of tests; the results were nearly flawless and his fame continued to grow.

In November 1973, he was jogging on his way to see some friends in New York City, and before he knew it, he had ended up in Ossining, thirty-six miles away, and it was a trip he "made" in twenty-five minutes. He had called his friends before he left his apartment; the person who drove him home that night confirmed that he was, in fact, giving Geller a lift back to New York City. The "flying" episode, much like the incident that had happened with Andrew Jackson Davis (see page 75), all those years ago, was thus proven to be legit.

Of this incident and others, Geller claims that his powers come from extraterrestrials, probably the same ones who gave him a "jolt" in the garden when he was a kid.

Geller has had some very high-profile friends. One of these was John Lennon, who Geller says "was very interesting, quite unusually gifted in the respect of visions." He also had a long-standing friendship with Michael Jackson, but it's unclear if this is still going on due to the controversy created by a series of specials about Jackson's life that Geller was interviewed for and that aired in 2003, painting the pop star in a not-too-flattering light.

Like any psychic, Geller has supporters and he has more than a few foes. Interestingly enough, not everyone in the magician world thinks Geller's a fraud. David Blaine has said that "Uri Geller is for real and anyone who doesn't recognize that is either deluding himself, or is a very sad person."

Naturally, not all are as supportive. Geller has many enemies and detractors. As Harry Houdini was to Margery the Medium (see page 165), so James Randi is to Uri Geller. Geller has been a nemesis of Randi's for years, and Randi is always quick to get a word of dissention in at the telepath's expense every opportunity he gets a chance to do so. "If Uri Geller bends spoons with divine powers, then he's doing it the hard way."

Regardless of the lack of support he gets from skeptics like Randi, Geller has been performing since the late 1960s and early 1970s. He made a very early appearance on the *Tonight Show* with Johnny Carson, which made him wildly famous in the United States; however, in 1973, when Randi and company alerted Carson and crew how to "set up safeguards to keep Geller from cheating," Geller could not perform. In fact, he failed miserably. Geller gave up after twenty minutes, explaining he was too tired to properly use his powers that night.

That event caused Geller much anguish and caused him to retreat for several years into a long depression. He finally fought back when he began suing writers and publishers who reported he was a fraud, saying they were tarnishing his reputation, but he lost those suits and was made to pay through the nose for them.

Eventually, Geller made a comeback on the *Tonight Show*, from whence he had been pushed into submission so many years before. This time, in addition to doing his trademark spoon bending, he was fixing broken watches and the like.

Randi, fed up with Geller, has been looking for an opportunity to see Geller retreat again. He's even challenged the psychic with his infamous million-dollar contest.

Geller says he has no more time for proving himself to those who don't have an open mind about believing in him. In fact, he wants nothing to do with the menacing magician. He's back with a positive attitude and he wants nothing to get in the way of that. He says, "My shows today are about motivation, inspiration, the power of self belief, the power of prayer, and the power of healing."

There's no room in his life for skeptics, for having to prove himself, for negativity. Geller stands on his beliefs and says to others, "Be positive, try always to be optimistic, always believe in yourself . . . be open-minded, not cynical and skeptical, because negativity is not going to get you anywhere. It's dreamers that make it in life, people with open-minded uninterrupted visions, they are the ones who have always succeeded."

LIBRARY OF CONGRESS

George Ivanovitch Gurdjieff
Mystic
(c. 1872–1949)

When my grandmother . . . was dying, my mother, as was then the custom, took me to her bedside, and I kissed her right hand, my dear now deceased grandmother placed her dying left hand on my head and in a whisper, yet very distinctly, said "Eldest of my grandsons! Listen and always remember my strict instruction to you: In life, never do as others do.

Either do nothing . . . or do something that nobody else does."

—George Ivanovitch Gurdjieff, of his
grandmother's dying words

From a very young age, George Ivanovitch Gurdjieff was aware of psychic powers. He knew he was different from others, and apparently, as her dying words indicate, so did his grandmother. Gurdjieff had no problem with her request to make a difference in the world, but he was going to do it on his own. Truth be told, Gurdjieff essentially denounced all his powers, but not before calling on them when he needed them in the pursuit of insight and enlightenment, that is.

Gurdjieff was born in Russian Armenia somewhere between 1866 and 1872; no one seems to know for sure. One thing that is known, however, is that Gurdjieff was a man of many powers—psychic and otherwise.

He was raised in an Orthodox Christian home, but the many other religious influences that were ever-apparent in the region in which he was raised made him believe from pretty early on that his religion was not the be-all and end-all—how could it be?

After the death of his grandmother, the young Gurdjieff had many experiences that led him to explore what else could be out there, even belief systems to which he had not yet been exposed. The death itself and the period of mourning that followed were a drain on the family, but then Gurdjieff did an experiment with himself: he decided to try and behave differently than what was expected of him. Instead of grieving at the gravesite, he circled the site, dancing and singing.

Later, his wisdom tooth was punched right out of his mouth during a fight at school, which gives an indication into how well he wanted to be—and was—accepted when he was a kid. These experiences were early windows into the insight about the world he would eventually gain.

By his mid-twenties, Gurdjieff was well aware of his abilities of telepathy and clairvoyance. Though he realized he had psychic powers, he felt that, for the most part, these would stand in the way of what he was to become, so he renounced them. Gurdjieff felt this was a huge first step he could make to control his own destiny. "As soon as I realized the sense of this idea, I was as if reincarnated," he said. "I got up and began to run around without knowing what I was doing, like a young calf. My mentation [*sic*] was unhindered."

Whether he used his powers of telepathy later, hypnotizing countless numbers of people into following the new ideas he posed, has been cause for great speculation that Gurdjieff was nothing but a fraud.

Once free of his "powers," Gurdjieff traveled the world in search of answers. He came away from his knowledge quest knowing one thing for certain: Humanity exists in a state of perpetual sleep. Gurdjieff said that man "must realize that he does not exist; he must realize that he can lose nothing because he has nothing to lose; he must realize his 'nothingness' in the full sense of the term."

In order to wake up, to really *live*, this sleep state must be transcended—and Gurdjieff made several interesting observations about how this could be done. Essentially, the crux of his teachings and message was that humanity must find a way to tap into the inner self, and only in that way could anyone ever claim that he or she was really *alive*. Conscience, consciousness, and sensation made up the formula on which development of human potential can fully be realized.

How could humanity "wake up"? Hypnotism was part of it. By being hypnotized, a person could connect to his or her essential yet dormant side. Controversially, some of the other ways included being totally obedient to a teacher who has already found the way to being awake. "This consciousness of one's nothingness alone can conquer the fear of subordination to the will of another," said Gurdjieff. He also explained this submission in this way, "A man does not realize that a subordination to which he consciously agrees is the only way to acquire a will of his own."

Other methods of self-awakening included constant self-observation and scrutiny, the performance of hard physical labor—even doing demeaning tasks—and intense emotionalism and exercise and dance routines that were designed to shock a person into the new state of awareness. In Russia, these were known as "sacred gymnastics"; when he settled in France, they were renamed "movements."

Like so many before him, Gurdjieff spent years getting to the bottom of his new philosophy. On top of incessant traveling, he studied Theosophy and other new belief systems, but still, nothing stuck. He was not satisfied. He believed that the real way was one that had not been tapped yet, and he decided he would establish his own school of thought based on the beliefs he considered to be essential.

In 1913, he settled in Moscow. There, he first introduced his philosophy, which he called the Fourth Way. He explained that the Fourth Way was in no way a conglomeration of teachings: it was the original way. While he was the one who developed it and brought it to moderns, he claimed that it had begun in Egypt, in 3000 BCE. No doubt, he needed to call on his psychic powers to find it as it had not been recorded anywhere before.

The Fourth Way is what shows humanity to use the ordinary to come to real life, to learn to live consciously without fear or regret. He called it "completely self-supporting and independent of other lines and it has been completely unknown up to the present time."

When turmoil began in Russia with all the controversy that had surrounded the life and death of Grigori Rasputin (see page 193), a supposed "spark" to the Russian Revolution, Gurdjieff realized that Russia, especially in the throes of a revolution, was no place for a mystic, so he decided to leave Moscow in 1917.

From there, he went to France and settled in Fontainebleau. There, he established the Institute for the Harmonious Development of Man in 1922, an institute that thrived until 1934.

Gurdjieff had many famous followers. Architect Frank Lloyd Wright was one of them. In fact, Wright had met his wife, Olgivanna, though the institute. She was a devout follower of Gurdjieff's philosophies and worked at the institute. Other famous followers included painter Georgia O'Keeffe and writer Katherine Mansfield, who spent the final months of her short life there.

Between 1935 and 1939, Gurdjieff sat with a special group he called "The Rope." This group was comprised of seven mostly famous female writers, which included Margaret Anderson, Kathryn Hume, and Solita Solano among them, who were mostly American. Gurdjieff's time with them was mostly informal; they met for casual lunches and dinners.

Though he was no longer teaching directly at the time, he still, for some reason, chose to work with this group of women. He encouraged the women to think of the experience as though they were mountain climbers, helping to pull each other up the side of a mountain. "You [are] very dirty . . . but have something very good— many people not got—very special."

Gurdjieff published several books. In 1950, *Beelzebub's Tales to his Grandson: An Impartial Criticism of the Life of Man* was a science-fiction novel with a message that people live too much in this world and all its trappings, and all but ignore the "inner self." In 1963, he published *Meetings with Remarkable Men*, the message of which was that "the present period of culture is, in the whole process of perfecting humanity, an empty and abortive interval." In 1978, this book was made into a film.

Gurdjieff did not have a lot of patience for the carnally and capitalitically obsessed United States, but he still had very devoted followers in America. Some of these followers established the Gurdjieff Foundation of New York in 1953 and another one in 1958 in San Francisco. Today, these organizations boast 5,000 followers, also known as "Gurdjieffians."

Even before his death in 1949, Gurdjieff had a bleak picture of modern man. "Humanity is at a standstill and from a standstill there is a straight path to downfall and degradation," he said. "Man is becoming a willing slave. He no longer needs chains. He begins to grow fond of his slavery, to be proud of it. And this is the most terrible thing that can happen to a man."

H

COURTESY OF CRAIG AND JANE HAMILTON-PARKER

Craig and Jane Hamilton-Parker
Mediums

Craig Hamilton-Parker (1954–)
Jane Hamilton-Parker (c. 1950s–)

*Jane and I were together in a previous life, and we
were destined to be together in this one. We have a
recurring dream in which we're being chased by
soldiers and dogs. It's during Mediaeval times and
we're running for our lives. . . . I think we're in France.*
                                    —Craig Hamilton-Parker

If you're in the mood for an out-of-this-world love story, look no
further. Now comes a tale of supernatural proportions: two mediums, lovers in past lives, each ending up burned by the wrong

person in this one, resigning never to love or marry again, then finding each other again—with a little help from not one but two lovable meddlers from beyond the grave. This is the story of Craig and Jane Hamilton-Parker, mediums and marrieds.

Having joined forces, the happy couple is now among the most talked about British celebrities. As two of the country's foremost psychics, they have become television stars, and Craig pens several columns and has written many books on the subject. Together with their remarkable accuracy in predictions, they have channeled such notables as Princess Diana among others. "It was medium Doris Stokes who predicted we would get together," Craig says. How that came about comes later.

Both Craig and Jane were aware of psychic abilities growing up. Jane says, "I was born with psychic abilities. As a child I saw auras and colours and could hear voices. . . . At my grandmother's house, I saw a woman wearing a long, old-fashioned nurses uniform. Her name was Alice. I said to my grandmother Ethel: 'I didn't know someone called Alice lived here.' She told me [Alice] was [the name of] her sister, a nurse who had been killed by a bomb during the war."

Craig had similar childhood experiences. He reports, "I could see lights around other people's heads. . . . I could read people's thoughts from an early age. . . . Also from an early age I started to see spirits."

But with all this psychic energy buzzing around them, neither ever pursued the gift—not right away, that is. Craig was a painter and then a graphic designer turned advertising executive; Jane was keeping herself busy with less-than-lofty pursuits. However, they maintained interest in spiritualism, and as adults, each attended groups. That interest was a very good thing, because it was at one of those meetings that their paths would finally cross in this lifetime.

It wasn't going to be instant kismet, however. At the time they met again, both were divorced with children from previous marriages; neither was interested in a second go around. But luckily, there were other forces at work.

Jane's spirit guide, her grandmother Ethel Wallis, saw that her granddaughter was about to find her soul mate again, and as a result, made sure that Jane attended the fateful meeting.

The deceased Doris Stokes, a medium who often came through to Craig, took it a step further. She reportedly channeled to Craig all the necessary details. Craig says that she told him he would soon meet his new wife and told him when and where. She even knew what her name would be. She got the first name right at least. The last name was off by one letter: Doris Stokes told him her name was "Jane Wallis" (Jane's grandmother's name), but at time they met, Jane was using her maiden name, Willis.

Lo and behold, on March 6, 1988, just as Stokes had told Craig, Jane and Craig attended the same meeting. The attraction was apparent and fierce, but the reluctance to take a chance again initially clouded the romance. Doubt was soon lifted, however; within three months, the mediums were married.

Everyone knows that marriage between regular mortals is hard enough. They say that after a while, you just *know* what your partner is thinking all the time, that you can read his or her mind. But how does it work when you're both psychic? How does it play out when you actually *can* read one another's minds? Craig says that "[t]elepathy works best when two people are in a cheerful frame of mind."

Married more than fifteen years, the Hamilton-Parkers currently live in the upscale neighborhood of Bishopstoke, Hampshire, England, with their daughter, Danielle, who is also psychic. They have also had psychic pets, including a beloved dog who was named William.

Part of what they claim is proof that they had been together in a previous life, along with Danielle, is that Craig says each of the three of them has a birthmark in the shape of a line, in the place where a guillotine may have beheaded them. He believes that the three of them were together, that they got into some sort of trouble and were all executed together.

Regarding predictions, Craig says that they don't come as if by magic, that a prediction is really deducted and developed, whether the prophet is aware of all this detective work or not. "A psychic can subconsciously calculate possible future events by an assessment of information available by the natural course of events and give probable forecasts," he explains. Whichever way they go about getting their information, it works.

Even with all the attention they get because of it, they're not always happy with the spectacle the media makes of them, and while they do a lot of television, they still wish that psychics were given more respect for their work. "Unless it's [psychics] being trashed by magicians, psychologists and journalists," Craig says, "television rarely makes serious programmes about the type of work we do."

One of the most memorable appearances they made was on a pay-per-view special that was hosting psychics who claimed to have talked with Princess Diana from beyond the grave. Jane had a spin that differed from what most of the psychics said, one that was decidedly less cynical and more romantic. "She did love Prince Charles," she reported, "and was so sad with the way things worked out."

Fame is all well and good, but in any kind of celebrity one enjoys, fame can get daunting. "Although we have this special gift, we're normal people and do the same everyday things as everyone else," Jane says. "If I'm shopping . . . people come up to me and say: 'Fancy seeing you here,' as if psychics don't eat."

The biggest convenience of a psychic marriage: No cell phones required. Craig says that he and Jane "are able to send out psychic thoughts to each other. The other day I popped to the shops to get some washing up liquid, and ended up coming back with some silver polish, too—which isn't the sort of thing you usually buy. It turned out Jane had sent me a thought asking for some."

John Holland
Medium
(c. 1964–)

Mediumship is about more than delivering messages.
It's about the confirmation that our "spirit" lives on,
once we leave our physical body. We are and always
will be connected to each other. Love is everlasting
and neither death nor time can ever separate us.

—John Holland, from JohnHolland.com

With his chiseled good looks and sparkling eyes, John Holland knows how to captivate a crowd. An animated, energized, and engaging speaker, the sexily professorial Holland packs seminars with admirers—but it's more than just wanting to be in the presence of this charming channeler, who really gets spectators involved. As Boston's premiere medium, Holland reports an accuracy rating of more than 70 percent.

A self-described "city kid" who grew up in a traumatizing, tumultuous alcoholic household, Holland feels these early experiences are part of what has made him psychic: He was often in the position to have to predict what was coming next to keep himself safe and sane. "As an adult, I look at my upbringing as an education and preparation for helping people," he explains. "I was learning what it's like to experience heartache and loss. . . . I was sort of a counselor even back then. I helped take care of my siblings at a very young age."

Any early psychic ability of which John may have been aware was generally chalked up to the survival method he had developed, so he never did anything about them. On top of the strife he experienced at home, he was having enough trouble fitting in with his classmates, very likely due, at least in part, to all that dysfunctional family baggage he was carrying around. Also, Holland could usually be found with his nose buried in metaphysical books, which only enhanced his reputation as "the weird kid."

When fate intervened and brought John's abilities to the undeniable surface, he was working, ironically when you consider his past, as a bartender. When he was thirty years old, he was involved in a near fatal car accident; at that time, the time of his near-death, he experienced a kind of rush wash over him. Once he recovered, he knew it was time to begin his real career, though he didn't jump into it immediately.

Finally, armed with his lifelong passion for metaphysics, John decided he needed to go to school to be properly trained to use his skills correctly. Between the ages of thirty-four and thirty-six, he went to England and attended the Arthur Findlay College, a world-famous training institute for psychics, which he playfully refers to as "Spirit Boot Camp." He wouldn't have wasted his time if he wasn't sure he had psychic powers, however. Holland doesn't believe it's possible to *become* a medium if you aren't actually born with the gift. He says that "anyone can learn to play the piano but that doesn't make them a pianist."

Returning to the States, the dynamic speaker with an uncanny knack for drawing people to him and for giving them what they want soon established himself as a world-class medium. People love attending a Holland appearance because he draws people in, and it's wholly on purpose. "There is a lot of audience participation when I lecture," he says. "I want people to be part of the experience."

A talent any good medium needs—aside from spirit channeling, naturally—is an ability to remain trustworthy and believable. When someone is suspicious because Holland can communicate with a spirit whose living language he does not speak, he explains that he can read any language spiritually, because they communicate without words, but with energy. No words are necessary. Holland is a pro at handling detractors, who generally don't bother with him. "I'm all about giving the evidence," he says. "I want clients to be skeptical. It's the cynics that get me."

When his clients are skeptical, he knows how to smooth the bumps of disbelief. If he's asked something like, "Why can't you bring Aunt Bertha through?" he typically has a calm, rational, and logical response. He'll take the stance that the spirits of your loved ones are "not with you twenty-four hours a day, seven days a week, but they are often there, when you need them most." So, much like in life, you can't summon spirits at your will and make them do tricks for you; free will is not something we lose when we die.

Holland also says that there is no change in people once they cross over. In other words, if you couldn't summon Aunt Bertha to you like a puppy dog when she was alive—and chances are, you'd probably get hit over the head with a well-stuffed pocketbook had you tried—there's no reason to think she'll be at your beck and call when she has so many other things with which to keep busy in the Great Beyond. He says that they don't become illuminated omniscient beings, that "[t]hey have the same personality and quirks."

In May 2003, he published his long-awaited first book, *Born Knowing: A Medium's Journey—Accepting and Embracing My Spiritual Gifts*. He writes candidly about his childhood and his psychic journey, as well as cuts through a lot of what he calls "psychic babble," to give readers a frank, down-to-earth look at the afterlife and his dealings with those who have passed into it.

Like many mediums, Holland doesn't think of the spirit world as being an actual place. "The Spirit World is . . . all around us," he says. "Everything is made of energy and vibrations. The energy of our physical world is slow and dense, whereas the Spirit World vibrates at a much higher rate . . . and the only thing that separates us is the frequency of the vibrations."

As far as who crosses over and to where, Holland says religion is not as important as people think it is. While it can help prepare a person for his or her passage to the spirit world, it doesn't matter which one is followed. In the end, if any particular religion has made a person better able to make that transition, it was a success.

As is the case among most mediums, as long as what they're doing is earnest and true and not a ploy to trick people into handing over money, Holland has nothing but respect for his contemporaries. There's no cutthroat battle going on, no psychic one-upmanship. He considers John Edward (see page 91)—probably his most equal contemporary—to be a "down-to-earth and brilliant medium."

Holland's secret of life success is that he believes in survival and making even the most terrible situations launch points for something much better—and that's never been truer for him than in the case of healing all the scars of his youth. "My childhood gave me strength as an adult," he says, "as I learned not to live in the past but to move on and live every day the best you can, for it's today that matters."

Daniel Dunglas Home
Physical Medium
(1833–1886)

*He must have been at least 80 feet from the
ground. . . . I saw Home's feet about six inches above
the window sill. He remained in this position for a
few seconds and then raised the window, glided into
the room feet first and sat down.*

>   —Lord Lindsay, a spectator astonished
>   by one of many of Daniel Dunglas
>   Home's levitation feats

Daniel Dunglas Home (pronounced HUME) dazzled many with his unexplainable feats and works of mediumistic magic in his lifetime, but if there's one claim to fame he shares with a small handful of others, he was never once in his career ever found to be fraudulent in any way. Many tried to trip him up but failed. Even years after Home's death, Harry Houdini himself said he would be able to replicate the events described in the epigraph above; he never did. Whether he couldn't figure out quite how to pull it off or he just lost interest is not known.

What is known, however, is that Home was one of the most enigmatic mediums of his lifetime—or any—and his antics continue to fascinate and enthrall well more than 100 years after his death, as well as of years of technological advances that still can't be used to explain some of the things Home was able to pull off. Famed parapsychologist John Beloff writes that Home was "the most celebrated medium of all time, judging by the number and impressiveness of the séances of which we have records and by the caliber of the observers whom he attracted in the many countries he visited."

147

In his lifetime, Home had many admirers, including Charles Dickens and Queen Victoria. He was apparently fun to have around, as he was possessed "of a highly emotional, joyous, childlike nature, full of generous impulses, and lavish affection to all comers." Not everyone was a fan, however. Allegedly, Home was nearly murdered by people who either flat out hated him or thought he was some kind of devil spawn on several occasions.

Born in Currie, near Edinburgh, Scotland, on March 20, 1833, Home was born into both poverty and instability. His father, William, claimed to be the illegitimate son of Alexander, the tenth earl of Home. His mother, Elizabeth, was a clairvoyant and a descendant of Highland seers.

Home's premonitions and precognitions began when he was a young child. At age four, he gave accounts to his parents of seeing pictures of future events. At age thirteen, after a childhood friend of his passed away, he reported talking with her in the street several days after the funeral.

There were a total of eight children in the family, which was more than the two parents could handle emotionally—forget the lack of means they had to support such a large family. To have a "visionary" in the fold was just too much. So Home was sent to America to live with his aunt and her family.

While Home was a teen growing up in the United States, strange things started taking place in his presence. Out of nowhere, furniture would move on its own, sometimes "chasing" other family members around the house. As nothing like these kind of events had occurred before Home came to live with her family, his aunt tried to have him exorcised. The priest to whom she took the boy said he was not possessed by Satan at all, but that Home had talents and was to use them to do God's work.

Home's aunt was not convinced and neither was the rest of the family. One day, as a settee was hunting down one of his cousins, who screamed around in terror, unable to get away from the crazy killer couch, Home's uncle looked to his nephew and noticed a maniacal smirk had formed on his face. That was enough for the family. The "satanic" Home was promptly kicked out of his aunt's house and left to fend for himself.

How he supported himself from this point is not exactly clear. Apparently, he never charged a penny for his psychic services, at this point and throughout his life; he only accepted gifts. Reports parapsychologist Alan Gauld, Home "never charged for his sittings, whatever gains he made from them being indirect and in the way of hospitality and gifts."

The guess is that he lived from house to house, relying on neighbors for warm meals and comfortable beds. In return, he provided them with a way to communicate with deceased loved ones.

Interestingly enough, Home held his séances in the brightest of light. Unlike most mediums, he didn't require the room to be dark to channel spirits.

In addition to bringing souls through from the other side, Home also levitated other people, as well as moved and levitated furniture. Really weird things happened in his presence. Musical instruments appeared and began to play; a hand appeared out of nowhere and began to write; raps and taps were heard and cool breezes were felt. Sometimes, the room even shook.

In 1852, around the age of nineteen, Home began levitating himself. It was this, out of all of the other things he did, that fell under the most scrutiny. He had even started to be tested as early as this, but nothing could be detected.

Home headed back to Britain in 1855, where he continued to make friends, influence people, and freak others way-the-hell out. Among the many amazing feats he pulled off, Home could stretch his body a foot taller than he was and handle burning hot coals right from the stove.

In the fall of 1855, he decided to travel and visited Italy, Holland, Russia, Prussia, and France. In Paris, he showed off his talents for Prince Murat, Napoléon III, and Empress Eugenie. This time, he called on one of his many talents: direct writing. Through Home,

Napoléon Bonaparte "wrote" his own name. The handwriting was verified by the world conqueror's grandson as being authentic.

Home lived in Rome for a while, and there he converted to Catholicism—if only briefly—and was received by Pope Pius IX. Eventually, Home began to unnerve the Catholics; he left Italy and his new religion behind and returned to Scotland.

Itchy to see the world, Home was soon off traveling again, this time to Russia, a country that had always held much fascination for him. In St. Petersburg, he met a wealthy Russian woman named Alexandrina, who also happened to be the goddaughter of the tsar. They were soon married.

In 1859, the couple returned to Britain, and soon were the proud parents of a boy, Gregorie.

Home continued to host countless séances, achieving much celebrity in his own country and beyond. He worked so much, in fact, that by the time he retired, it was reported that he probably had conducted 1,500 séances in his life.

Home and Alexandrina lived essentially on her money and had many of their expenses taken care of through the many "gifts" of supporters and friends. So when Alexandrina died in 1862, the money quickly ran out. To support himself and his young son, Home still didn't rely on his séances for income, but he now gave lectures and wrote the two-volume book *Incidents in My Life* (1863–72) to generate revenue.

Home began to feel burned out by his psychic work, so, to take a break, he went back to Rome to study to become a sculptor. Italy never held the same enthusiasm for Home that he held for it, and soon enough, he was in trouble again. Just a few months into his classes, Home was charged with sorcery and asked to leave Italy. For good.

Returning to Scotland in April 1864, some friends of Home's formed the Spiritual Athenaeum as a way to support Home financially. They wanted to keep him in Britain where they felt he belonged.

The most memorable feat Home ever performed was for a couple of doubting nobles, Lord Lindsay and Lord Adare. On December 13, 1868, Home "floated" out of a window from one house and into the window of another, where Lindsay and Adare sat waiting for him and greeted him with unbridled astonishment. "He must have been at least 80 feet from the ground," exclaimed Lord Lindsay of the remarkable feat.

Home was suspected of using chloroform and hypnosis to trick his guests, but no evidence was ever found of this. Additionally, he immediately took the guests to the window through which he had slipped in the other house, which was open just barely a foot wide. Home explained that he had floated out the window sideways, head first.

When asked how he felt about his unique abilities, especially the levitation, he said he was not afraid. "Since the first time, I have never felt fear," Home explained. "Should I, however, have fallen from the ceiling of some of the rooms in which I have been raised, I could not have escaped serious injury. I am generally lifted up perpendicularly; my arms frequently become rigid and are drawn to my head as if I were grasping the unseen power which slowly raises me from the floor."

Home continued to be scrupulously tested, but he was never shown up. As Beloff states, "The hard fact, against which would-be debunkers can only bang their heads, is that, for more than twenty years, Home gave regular sittings, sometimes more than one a week, at which in good illumination (usually gaslight) a large table would be levitated to shoulder height or higher and that in no case was he ever detected . . . using sleight-of-hand."

In 1871, Home underwent some of the most challenging tests of his career, under the direction of Sir William Crookes, a reputable scientist known to eat false psychics for breakfast.

Crookes conducted a slew of experiments with Home, giving the gifted man various tasks and tests and gauging his ability based on his success in fulfilling the requests.

First, Crookes challenged Home to move a spring balance, which was at the other end of the room. He did. Next, Crookes asked him to play an accordion that had been enclosed in a copper cage. Calling again on his telekinetic powers, Home played the accordion. As a special bonus, Home did a trick with a piece of coal, which others had seen him do before. He reached into the stove, pulled out a handful of hot coals, and rolled them around in the palm of his hand. When Crookes later examined the area for burns, none were found.

The skeptic was converted, writing in his conclusions that Home was "connected with the human organization, which for convenience may be called the Psychic Force."

In 1871, Home married another wealthy woman from Russia, heiress Julie de Gloumeline. By this time, he was ready to slow down. For one, because he had been performing séances and other psychic feats for years and it was time for a break, but also because he had developed tuberculosis and simply could not muster up the energy to work as he had. He retired and moved with his family to the Mediterranean in 1873.

In June 1886, the tuberculosis won, and Home was buried at St. Germain-en-Laye in France.

Home's wife, Julie de Gloumeline Home, was not finished with his work, and after his death, she published two books about her husband and his life: *D.D. Home: His Life and Mission* (1888) and *The Gift of D.D. Home* (1890).

Years after his death, the controversy over Home's abilities flourishes, but the answers have never been found and he remains the only psychic ever able to escape completely the stigma of "fraud."

CORBIS

Peter Hurkos
Psychic Sleuth
(1911–1988)

I see pictures in my mind like a television screen.
When I touch something, I can tell what I see.

—Peter Hurkos

Crime solver, painter, gardener, family man, and psychic. All these labels correctly describe Peter Hurkos, a sleuth who relied on supernatural skills to solve cases and, in his career, worked on twenty-seven murders in seventeen countries.

Most prominent in the 1950s, 1960s, and 1970s, Hurkos was known as "the Man with the Radar Brain," and his name is forever connected with helping to solve such high-profile cases as the Boston

Strangler killings and the Manson family murder spree. But all in all, he was just a regular guy who happened to have a gift and made little fuss about it.

Born on May 21, 1911, in Dordrecht, Holland, Hurkos didn't have the typical childhood of your average adult psychic. He did not have any special visions or premonitions; his reality was much the same as anyone else's, even as he grew into adulthood and throughout his twenties.

When he turned thirty, everything changed. It wasn't as if one day he was average and the next, he could all of a sudden see things others could not. In 1941, while painting a house in his native Holland, Hurkos fell off a ladder, plummeting four stories and landing square on his head.

He should have died, but he didn't. Instead, he suffered a brain injury and remained in a coma for three days at the Zuidwal Hospital.

When he awoke from his coma, things were decidedly different. He knew things he could not possibly have known about; throughout his recovery, he came to realize that his life was changed for good.

In the coming years, Hurkos began making a name for himself in Holland, and word began to spread throughout the world about his uncanny psychic ability.

In 1956, he met an American doctor, Andrija Puharich, who wanted to bring him back to his laboratory in Glen Cove, Long Island, New York, to test Hurkos's special talents. Hurkos readily agreed and spent the next two and a half years being rigorously tested by the persistent scientist. With an accuracy rating of more than 90 percent, Puharich had no choice but to deem Hurkos the "real thing."

Hurkos decided to stay in America after this testing, where he gained more and more prominence. He got married and started a family. He dabbled in painting canvases and unwound from his hectic lifestyle with gardening. He also started solving crimes.

Hurkos's main talent was "psychometry." This essentially meant that he could tell all about a person by touching something that belonged to that person. As Hurkos explained, "Sometimes people try to trick me, but I touch their object . . . I see pictures in my mind about what's happening . . . then I tell them."

This unusual skill seemed ideally suited for detective work, and Hurkos answered the call many times.

In 1963, the Boston Strangler case had police detectives baffled. There were about thirteen women strangled in Boston between 1962 and 1964, but the killer evaded the police at every turn. Hurkos got involved and provided many leads as to who the real killer was. When the police brought in Albert De Salvo as the killer, however, Hurkos was not convinced. De Salvo didn't match up with any of Hurkos's feelings, and he told the police time and time again that they had the wrong man.

Years later—years after the deaths of both Hurkos and De Salvo—it was suspected that the wrong man was convicted and that the killer might still be at large.

One of the biggest cases Hurkos was ever involved in was the Manson family murders of Sharon Tate and her houseguests the LiBiancas in the summer of 1969. These brutal murders, Hurkos told police, were committed by a group led by a man named "Charlie" who wore a beard. In prison for a shoplifting offense, Susan "Sexy Sadie" Atkins blabbed that she and her "family" were behind the killings, under the direction of "Charlie," who, as it so happened, had been sporting a beard when they brought him in.

One of the main things for which Hurkos was, unfairly, criticized was that he charged for his work. Other psychic sleuths never asked a penny, except to cover expenses. Hurkos, on the other hand, was known to charge fees of $2,500 for his work, *plus* expenses. He didn't give in to his critics, however. "When you have a gift, you don't have to be afraid to prove it," Hurkos said. And also, if you rely on your gift to feed and clothe your family, and if it takes up the majority of your time, and is, in fact, your job, why shouldn't you get paid?

Hurkos wasn't at all a fan of faux psychics, who diminished the work and efforts of those whom Hurkos felt were "for real"—like himself—and he warned people always to be cautious. "If you ever go to a psychic, don't ask any questions or give any clues," he advised. "If they are psychic, they should be able to tell what the problem is."

For all those who criticized him, however, many embraced him. He was a frequent guest of many talk-show personalities of the 1970s and 1980s, including Merv Griffin, Johnny Carson, Ed Sullivan, and even Geraldo Rivera. His life and work was also the subject of a proliferation of documentaries and films, and he even made cameo appearances in films and television shows.

On top of that, there have not been many psychics who have been supported by the Catholic Church for their work, but Hurkos was one of them. On a visit to the Vatican in the 1950s, he had an audience with the pope, who encouraged his work. "I hope you will always use your God-given Gift for the betterment of mankind," Pope Pius XII told him. "Use it as an instrument to touch people, to help them."

Peter Hurkos was the author of three books: *Psychic* (1967), *The Psychic World of Peter Hurkos* (1970), and *Peter Hurkos: I Have Lived Many Lives* (1976). He died on June 1, 1988.

J

Elizabeth Joyce
Clairvoyant, Medium, Healer
(c. 1950s–)

*As the light increases, we see ourselves to be worse
than we thought. We are amazed at our former
blindness as we see issuing forth from the depths of our
heart a whole swarm of shameful feelings. . . . Bear in
mind, for your comfort, that we only truly perceive the
depth of our malady when the cure begins.*

—Francois Fenelon (1651–1715), as quoted
on Elizabeth Joyce's Web site

It's remarkable when a set of twins is born into any given family;
when two sets of identical sisters are born into the same family, a
more appropriate word might actually be "miraculous." And if

you're prone to believe that that kind of magic can rub off and manifest itself into those twins, then you're sure to take psychic Elizabeth Joyce, Ridgewood, New Jersey's answer to Jeane Dixon (see page 86), at her word.

Joyce's father was a master bridge player, who taught the game to others for more than thirty years. Her mother was a school teacher. Elizabeth was born into the second duo of daughters; the older sisters did TV commercials, and she and her twin appeared on *American Bandstand*.

Today, married for the third time and mother of two sons, Joyce's psychic talents are very much in tune with her family ties. In fact, the point she realized she had psychic powers was after she had been involved in a head-on collision with a drunk driver, with her son in the car, and had an out-of-body experience. In recovery, she all of a sudden had answers she never had before.

Other psychic experiences involving her family abound. For instance, she knew her sister was going to be involved in a near-fatal accident when she had a dream about it. In the dream, she was able to save her twin; in life, when she got the call about the accident, she felt as though she herself might stop breathing until her mother assured Joyce that her sister would be okay.

She says that she knew her father was going to die, even though he had been perfectly healthy the last time she'd seen him and there was no indication that his time was growing short. She jumped in her car with a friend in the middle of the night and drove all night, making it to her parents' home before her mother was even able to call her. Joyce claims that she also eased her mother's transition to the other side in 1991.

The most tragic family connection in her psychic career, however, came in her work as a psychic detective and she was helping police to find her missing stepson. "The most difficult time this ever happened to me was when I located the body of my dead stepson in 1979," she said of the event. "That was devastating."

Today a psychic and a teacher of metaphysics, Joyce is one of the most educated practitioners in her milieu. A graduate of Quiet

Decisions Hypnotherapy and Behavior Modification in New York, she also studied at the Louise Hay Institute in Santa Monica, and has spent time with Deepak Chopra.

She has a very focused mission in her work. "I help people put positive thoughts in their minds so they can work through issues or cope with disaster," she says. "I always try to leave my clients with hope and some active steps to create changes in their lives. I go into past-life and present-life regression work. Many of us suffer from post-traumatic experiences, co-dependency, negative habits and responses as well as catastrophic experiences."

In September 1997, *American Woman* magazine named her one of the top twenty psychics in the country, but one of her most distinguished distinctions was bestowed on her in 1998. That year, she was named psychic of the year by ABC News for predicting the President Bill Clinton and Monica Lewinsky affair.

Joyce's prediction was published in *Fate* magazine well before the outbreak of the scandal in September 1997. "A dark-haired woman named Veronica will upset the Clinton Administration in early 1998, and Clinton may not give the State of the Union Address," it read. "An angry blonde will bring forth the truth. This will be verified by others later and Clinton will be Impeached late in the year."

As you might guess from this prediction, it's Joyce's prophecies that have drawn the most attention to her. Those that have come to pass, as presented on her Web site, are enough to convert many skeptics to believing. Taken from her Web site, dated October 6, 2001, she predicted: "Chandra Levy is dead. Strangled. Her body will be found, under water, near some boats. She was murdered by a blond haired man. His sandals will be located near the crime scene shortly." Chandra Levy's body was finally found, strangled, and her killer is still at large.

And then there's this terrifying prophecy, dated November 2000: "Expect disaster in New York City, Washington, D.C., and Los Angeles in the fall months right after school begins in 2001," it reads. "A bomb is headed for each city, with thousands of lives lost. Tall buildings are the target, as well as the White House, and they will fall down like a feather!"

Additionally, Joyce knew after Elizabeth Smart was kidnapped that she was alive, and posted the information on her Web site. Joyce said that the kidnapper was a workman in the Smart house, that he wore a long beard, and that Smart would return alive in a year or so and write about her experience.

Some prophecies never came to pass. Among other mispredictions, she said that in January 2002 the water of the San Francisco Bay would be poisoned and that in the last quarter of 2001, "Civil unrest sweeps through Mexico in the wake of a political scandal and President Bush plans to make Mexico our 51st state."

You only need to open a newspaper to see that these events have not occurred; however, Joyce claims that these mispredictions—and others—may still yet come to pass. "I have received complaints, especially from the Skeptics [*sic*], about my timing of events," she says. "They never mentioned the accuracy of the predictions, only my error in timing. Or they pick out something that did not happen from something that did, and embellish on it. . . . There are to [*sic*] many variables when predicting timing, especially the power of human decisions." So if something she said would happen hasn't happened yet, she feels that it will, just in its own time.

In those prophecies that are yet to come, Joyce says that Christie Todd Whitman could run for Vice President in 2004. She's also on board with psychics like Ruth Montgomery (see page 175) and Edgar Cayce (see page 61), with the prophecy that the earth will shift on its axis in 2012 and that a walk-in president, who will likely be elected in 2004, will be the one to help humanity deal with the many calamities and crises that arise.

Like her fellow prognosticators, Joyce says we can't avert the shifting, no matter what we do, but we can avoid other cataclysmic events from taking place, she says, by "living a good life and loving others, including ones who are different from us, is a good way to begin. Send forth love instead of judgment, hate and condemnation."

K

AP WORLDWIDE

The Amazing Kreskin
(a.k.a. George Joseph Kresge Jr.)
Mentalist
(1935–)

I do not call myself a mind reader, because that
implies I can totally penetrate the process of the
human brain. I prefer to describe myself as a
thought reader.

—The Amazing Kreskin

Some psychics are born that way, some are found out later in life, and some, like The Amazing Kreskin, are actually *made*, soaking up every bit of information that exists on the subject of psychic

161

phenomena and using the knowledge to forge some miracle on their own.

The former George Joseph Kresge Jr. has performed the world over for royalty and presidents, for common folk and powerful persons alike. In a career that's spanned more than fifty years, he's made more than 500 television appearances and performed hundreds of live engagements. He performs some magic tricks in his act, explaining that "[t]he ESP factor needs a solid mental foundation to be successful. Once the audience members become mystified, they are more susceptible to suggestion."

Kreskin's not just an entertainer, however. He's used his amazing gifts to make some pretty eerie predictions, as we shall soon see.

So secure is Kreskin in his skills, that he offers up a reward of $50,000 of his own money for anyone who can prove that not only is he not for real, but also that he enlists help through assistants to make his illusions seem like the real thing.

Born January 12, 1935, in Montclair, New Jersey, Kreskin changed his name when he started getting serious about his work when he was barely out of adolescence. In fact, he has even legally changed his first and middle names to "The" and "Amazing."

He first learned he had special gifts early in his childhood when he could recover hidden objects. At the age of five, during a game of "hot" and "cold," he blew the other children away as nothing could be hidden from him; he could find anything.

From that point, his sense of telepathy developed. Inspired by the "Marmaduke the Magician" comic strip, he began learning all about magic and mentalism, and was soon entertaining neighborhood children with his fantastic feats of telepathy and lost-item recovery. At age eleven, he read the entire psychology section in his local library and added another gimmick to his act: hypnotism. Soon, he was hypnotizing all his friends and classmates, and in performance, he began billing himself as the "World's Youngest Hypnotist."

As a teenager, he got even more seriously involved in hypnotism. When he was a sophomore in high school, having grown out of the "World's Youngest Hypnotist" description, he needed something to call himself for an upcoming show. He came up with "Kreskin" by adding on another K, and, in paying homage to Houdini, topped off the name with an "in."

The Amazing Kreskin hit the television airwaves for the first time with the *Steve Allen Show* in the early 1960s. By the early 1970s, he had made his first of many appearances on the *Tonight Show*—and says Johnny Carson's "Carnac the Magnificent" character is based on him.

After proving his ilk to television producers, Kreskin got the chance to do his own show. *The Amazing World of Kreskin* was made and broadcast in Canada from 1971 to 1975. During the show's five-and-a-half-season run, with twenty-six episodes per season, Kreskin continued to entertain and amaze with his mix of magic and telepathy.

Kreskin is the author of eight books about his life and work, including *The Amazing World of Kreskin* (1973), *Kreskin's Mind Power Book* (1986), *Kreskin's Fun Ways to Mind Expansion* (1984), *Secrets of the Amazing Kreskin* (1991), *How to be a Fake Kreskin* (1996), and *The Amazing Kreskin's Future with the Stars* (2001).

In the most recent of these books, Kreskin made a point to explain that "the enemy is using the most invisible and insidious of tactics—that of terrorism. The gravest danger that the world has faced in the last 100 years will be showing its ugly face before long." He warned that "[w]ith the ominous possibilities of biological warfare, safety zones will inevitably be setup in schools and government buildings."

Despite his success with prophecy and telepathy, Kreskin doesn't necessarily like to be referred to as a psychic—not a mind reader, more of a thought reader. "I am not a mind reader and I am not a hypnotist," he explains.

Pushing seventy years old, the unstoppable Kreskin continues to do all kinds of television and radio shows. Every year on New Year's Day, on *CNN Today*, he releases his predictions. These have included that Hillary Clinton would run for the New York Senate and that the Yankees would lose the series in 2001. He also predicts who the Oscar winners will be each year and more.

Freakily enough, in January 2001, he predicted that "by September or October, there would be two major plane crashes." Of course, plenty of stuff has not come true, including countless predictions surrounding UFOs. One year, Kreskin said that "[i]n May or June of this year the largest sighting to date in the past century will take place in the Nevada desert." To date (2004), this UFO had not been sighted.

Kreskin, an avid seeker of paranormal knowledge who boasts the "largest private collection of books in parapsychology in the world," says it's important to understand that his predictions don't just come to him: He says that he studies thoughts and vibrations, and that his predictions come to him through careful analysis and deduction of these vibrations and thoughts.

Whatever his methods, Kreskin is generally regarded as being fairly accurate and reputable with the information he puts out there. In the words of *Newsweek* columnist Gersh Kuntzman, "The Amazing Kreskin remains America's flesh-and-blood Magic 8-ball."

LIBRARY OF CONGRESS

Margery the Medium
(a.k.a. Mina Crandon)
Medium, Clairvoyant
(1888–1941)

Few mediums can have caused quite as much havoc in their time as Margery. The American Society for Psychical Research split in two on her account.

—J. Beloff, The Relentless Question:
Reflections on the Paranormal (1990)

If an award were ever given out for the sexiest medium ever, Mina Crandon would certainly have clinched it. When Mina conducted séances, she typically greeted sitters wearing little more than a sheer nightie with bedroom slippers over silk stockings. Why? Not to distract her sitters, she claimed, as more than a few detractors have speculated. Rather, by wearing as little clothing as possible she could prove, without a doubt, that there was nothing "up her sleeve."

Skeptics had another story. They wholly believed that the provocative attire was a ploy for taking attention away from any fraud she might be perpetrating. Magician Harry Houdini, perhaps Mina's greatest nemesis, speculated in his most vicious attacks that Mina peeled off her nightie during her sittings, conducting séances in the buff. Worse yet, rumors ran rampant that Mina sometimes actually "seduced" investigators into believing she was the real thing.

Whether she intentionally used her sex appeal to her advantage or not, Mina was, as one nonbeliever said, "too attractive for her own good." On the flip side of Houdini's guile, however, there was speculation that the famed magician might even himself have been in love with the blue-eyed bain of his existence, and he often cautioned others to "avoid falling in love with the medium." Of course, this has never been proven.

Whether it was her good looks or dubious supersenory skills, controversy courted Mina; as much energy as Houdini put in to showing her up as a charlatan, others staked as much—in the form of their very reputations—on her veracity and validity. The controversy caused a giant rift in the psychic community that could only just begin to be repaired after her death. On top of that, Mina's fame and notoriety brought the spiritualist movement back out of the shadows, where it had been slowly withering away and dying since Maggie Fox's confession (see page 126) in 1888. Ironically, 1888 is the same year Mina was born.

Mina Stinson grew up on a farm in Ontario. She was a gifted child, who counted among her many skills a talent in music. Mina played many musical instruments, including the piano, cornet, and cello. One talent she did not count among the many she had growing up, however, was psychic ability. Unlike most every other psychic in this collection, her talents did not surface until adulthood—until she was past thirty, even.

But psychic talent was in her family. According to the Noah's Ark Web site, Mina's older brother, Walter, whom she adored and to whom she was closest in her family, had psychic ability, and these abilities would show up long after he was dead.

When she was sixteen or seventeen, Mina left Ontario and moved to Boston to pursue a music career. While she waited for her big break, she worked all kinds of odd jobs, from secretary to ambulance driver. In 1911, when Mina was twenty-three, her brother Walter was killed in a railroad accident. Though devastated, she decided not to return to Ontario.

Mina endured a bad marriage to a local grocer, Earl P. Rand, whom she divorced in 1918. That same year, she met Dr. Le Roi Goddard Crandon, a prestigious Boston surgeon and professor—and *Mayflower* descendant—who was more than ten years her senior, and married him quickly after her divorce was final.

The Crandons took up residence in the elegant Beacon Hill section of the city, at 11 Lime Street, an address that still stands and attracts intrigued visitors today. To all appearances, the Crandons enjoyed a successful marriage; that Le Roi was a philanderer and possibly abusive didn't surface until years after they were both dead. For all intents and purposes, they lived a comfortable lifestyle and were a very popular couple with many friends and social obligations.

Into this halcyon world, Mina's psychic ability would soon creep—although it wasn't she who brought it out. Not really. Dr. Crandon essentially controlled their lives. He decided whom they would be friends with and what they would be interested in, and so it comes as no surprise that it was Crandon who introduced them to spiritualism on a whim. He had been doing some reading on the subject and was intrigued, so he decided they would try their hand at it. Earlier, Mina had seen a psychic who had told her she had abilities, but she had ignored that. Essentially, Mina was not interested; she simply went along with her husband.

On May 27, 1923, the Crandons invited friends over for a séance. Everyone was very serious—almost too serious—sitting around in the dark, waiting for the spirits to visit. It was almost too much for the lighthearted, girlish Mina to take, and she was struck with the giggles. "They were all so solemn about it that I couldn't help laughing," she explained.

Dr. Crandon didn't even have a moment to chide his insolent little wife before strange things started to happen. Most notably, the table they had been using for the séance began to tilt in response to answers to questions they asked. Crandon wanted to get to the bottom of it, and therefore had each member of the party sit at the table alone to see who was the one who had the power to make the table move.

The table moved for no one until the last sitter: Mina was the medium.

They all got serious, including the once-giggly Mina. This fateful event led 11 Lime Street to become séance central. The Crandons conducted countless séances, and Mina gained notoriety. Hundreds pined to sit in the house's dark rooms and witness the mysterious happenings channeled by the doctor's wife, from raps and bumps, to flashes of light, to unexplained breezes.

The most interesting aspect of these séances were the disembodied voices that came from Mina. That's not exactly accurate—the voices never actually came from Mina at all, but from around her. Eerily, voices could come through as far as eight feet away from where she was sitting and speak their messages to the anxious sitters.

The most significant voice that came through, however, belonged to Mina's beloved older brother Walter. Walter spoke from the other side as a street-talking smart-ass, just as he had been in life, which validated that it was, indeed, Walter. It didn't matter, of course, that no one in Boston even knew Walter except for Mina herself, so no one would ever know what Walter was really like to prove that he was, in fact, coming through.

Of course, the skeptics didn't believe the "voices" were spirits at all, but the work of a skilled ventriloquist. Walter put an end to those doubts. During a séance in 1923, an annoyed Walter demanded everyone in the room fill their mouths with water: Mina, Le Roi, the sitters—everyone. With everyone having their mouths incapacitated for speech, Walter still managed to talk, and as clearly as ever.

As Mina's ability became more and more pronounced and famous, it started to become a wee bit uncomfy for the prestigious doctor to be associated with so much speculative science. A friend and staunch supporter of Mina, J. Malcolm Bird, who also happened to be the associate editor of *Scientific American* at the time, recommended that Mina change her name to "Margery the Medium." That is the moniker Mina is, even today, most identified by.

As is the case with any successful psychic, Margery had her share of supporters and detractors. Bird was a strong supporter, and also, many say, an admirer and even a lover of the sexy medium, but he wasn't the only high-profile supporter. Arthur Conan Doyle was also an enthusiastic fan.

Harry Houdini led the dissenters. Said Houdini, "I am willing to be convinced." He insisted that his "mind is open, but the proof must be such as to leave no vestige of doubt that what is claimed to be done is accomplished only through or by supernatural power."

Of course, Houdini had his own well-known issues with mediumship. It would be especially evident in his trying to disprove Margery that the window of Houdini's mind could only be "opened" so far; he decided, some say, to only open it a crack, and that was the limit.

In 1921, the editors of *Scientific American* cooked up a psychic ability contest and assembled a panel of judges to assess what made for a true medium and what made for a fraud. The contest was made public in December 1922, promising to award "$2,500 to the first person who produces a psychic photograph under test conditions" and an additional "$2,500 to the first person who produces psychic manifestation of the other character . . . to the full satisfaction of these judges." Margery agreed to enter, but already affluent, she said she would not accept the money if she won. What she was looking for was validity and substantiation; what she would find was more turmoil than she had ever imagined possible.

The selected judges included psychical researcher Walter Franklin Pierce, occult writer Hereward Carrington, cinematographer Daniel Comstock, and psychology professor William McDougall. In November 1922, when Houdini became aware of the contest, he tried to get in as a judge. At first, the organizers did not want Houdini, who was a known skeptic pest. He was eventually invited to join the others, but then wasn't notified till months later that the testing had begun. Houdini was furious and wrote scathing letters to the magazine; Bird (who had wanted to disqualify Houdini) wrote back to him explaining they did not want to bother him while he was on tour, further angering the volatile magician.

Now hell-bent on defrauding Margery, Houdini proclaimed that if he could not prove her a fraud, he'd return his $1,000 judge's fee. So incensed by her was he, in fact, that he later even published a book on the events of the testing: *Houdini Exposes the Tricks Used by the Boston Medium Margery* (1924).

On July 23, 1923, the official test of Margery's ability was conducted at the Crandons' home. The first feat that Margery was to perform was to make a bell ring, without her or anyone else touching it. Her hands and feet were held by those surrounding her so there could be no question about her physically ringing the bell.

Earlier that day, Houdini had tightly tied a garter just below his knee, cutting off the circulation to the lower part of his leg to increase sensitivity. "As the séance progressed I could distinctly feel her ankle slowly and spasmodically sliding as it pressed against mine while she gained space to raise her foot off the floor and touch the top of the box," he explained.

One down, two to go.

In another test, Walter actually moved matter, at Houdini's request. A megaphone had been levitating vis-à-vis the spiteful sprite, and he asked his sister where he should throw it. Houdini asked him to throw the megaphone to him, which is what appeared to happen, but Houdini had it all figured out. He concluded that earlier, when her hands had been free, Margery held the megaphone on her head. When Houdini asked that it be thrown to him, he determined that all she needed to do was to snap her head forward, and voilà: the megaphone ended up at its destination. "This is the 'slickest' ruse I have ever detected," he bemused, "and it has converted all skeptics."

Strike two.

For the third test, Margery was put in a cabinet that Houdini designed specifically to keep her arms and legs contained and so that her movements could be easily monitored. While she was in the cabinet, Walter was asked to ring the bell. Nothing happened. Inspection of the crate revealed that a pencil eraser was jammed into the bell mechanism, preventing it from ringing.

Another thing that threw suspicion in her direction was that a small ruler was found in the cabinet after the séance, which Houdini determined was the source of the tapping. Margery denied even knowing the ruler was in there, but she was not believed. Interestingly enough, years after Houdini's death, James Collins, a former assistant of Houdini's, said he was told to plant the ruler. "I chucked it in the box meself. The boss told me to do it. He wanted to fix her good."

Whether this was true or not or whether Houdini himself had jammed the eraser into the bell mechanism was never fully proven, but at least one conclusion can be drawn: Houdini did not enter the judging objectively and could very well then have uttered his conclusion that "everything which took place at the séances I attended was a deliberate and conscious fraud" before taking even his first step into the Crandons' home.

The contest was nullified when the test results proved inconclusive and with that, Margery's mediumistic credibility began to slowly unravel. But the Crandon séances continued and drew many believers. In 1924, spirits Margery channeled began to take "teleplasmic manifestations"—during her séances, ectoplasm poured from every imaginable orifice and molded itself into "limbs."

By the mid-1920s, the Margery controversy was in full swing—

and continued even after Houdini's death in 1926. Detractors, such as J. B. Rhine publicly denounced Margery. Supporters, most notably Arthur Conan Doyle, defended her incessantly: Doyle even took out a full-page newspaper ad, with a simple message on it: "J. B. Rhine is an ass." Dr. E. J. Dingwall attended twenty-nine sittings and could find no evidence of fraud. However, the conclusions he published six months after his sittings were "inconclusive." His final conclusion, "The phenomena witnessed by me, could, I think, be duplicated by normal methods."

Furious controversy sparked more furious investigation. Soon, the American Society for Psychical Research was divided right down the middle between those who supported Margery and those who did not. It would remain divided until 1941, the year Margery died.

The most incriminating case for fraud by Margery could be made by a scam that was proven to be utter rubbish in the 1930s. Spirit Walter had by this time become more sophisticated physically—even leaving his fingerprint in a wad of dental wax left on the dining room table. When the fingerprint was absolutely identified as that of Dr. Frederick Caldwell, Margery's dentist, it was the beginning of the end.

Skeptics consider this the defining moment in exposing Margery as a fake; supporters believe she was set up, that the dental wax scam was not something of which she was aware, and was probably set up by Dr. Crandon, thinking he was clever enough to shut the skeptics up for good.

Whatever the case, Margery never fully bounced back. When her husband died in 1939, it was just a matter of time before she came fully undone. The stress of the controversy she had caused, the now nearly universal belief that she was a sham, and the death of her husband led her right to a nervous breakdown. She drank herself to death by November 1, 1941, never having confirmation that at least some people still believed in her.

"NINETEENTH-CENTURY MENTALIST PERFORMING," LIBRARY OF CONGRESS

Marvelous feats in Mind Reading.

Wolf Messing

Mentalist

(1899–1974)

The most beautiful thing we can experience is the mysterious. It is the source of all true art and science.

—Albert Einstein

Born on September 10, 1899, in Poland, Wolf Messing was one of the most talented mind readers of all time. In his life, he became so famous for his talents that he even had Adolf Hitler and Joseph

Stalin interested in his abilities. Stalin was intrigued and played lots of games with Messing to test his talents; Hitler put a price on his head.

Whether loved or reviled, one thing remained constant: Messing had an impeccable knack for, well, "messing" with minds, and as such, earns a place of distinction among the greatest psychics of all time.

Some of the less politically charged things that Messing used his mind manipulation skill for could be pretty innocuous and maybe just a little mischievous. For example, he once used his mind to convince a train conductor that he actually did have a ticket when Messing didn't have enough money to afford one for himself.

When he was a boy, he had made the acquaintance of a man who gave him a chance to take his talents to the stage, where he amazed spectators with his abilities. He was tested by both Albert Einstein and Sigmund Freud, who were fascinated by the young man's talent.

But soon, he got too smart for his own good and put his own life in jeopardy. Around the onset of World War II, he had been giving performances in Vienna and then Berlin, and had started to tread on some pretty dangerous ground.

Wolf Messing was Jewish, and this was not a good time to be so, especially in Austria and Germany. Both of his parents, and several of his relatives, were killed in the Maidenek death camp. Around this time, in performance, Messing predicted that Hitler would be dead in 1945. Hitler put a price on Messing's head: 200,000 marks.

Needless to say, Messing had to get away from Hitler and fast. He tried to flee to Russia in 1939, but was captured. That wasn't a problem for the resourceful mentalist. He soon managed to escape by playing mind tricks with the guards. He eventually tricked them into entering his cell, got himself on the outside, locked them up, and ran to Russia.

Within six months, Messing had made a name for himself in Russia, where he married and lived out his life.

His involvement in politics was not over yet, however. Stalin became intrigued by Messing and began to play a series of games with him.

In the first test, Messing was to enter Stalin's country home without being stopped. Lo and behold, on the appointed day, when the guards would be tipped off that Messing was going to try and get in, Messing slipped right through. How? He used mind tricks to successfully fool the guards into thinking he was a particularly menacing head of military, the head of the secret police, whom everyone feared, and a good friend of Stalin's at that.

Stalin was utterly intrigued and wanted to see Messing's gifts in action again. This time he ordered Messing to rob a bank. Messing walked into the bank without a weapon and walked out with a bag of money. How did he pull this one off? This time, he made a mental suggestion to the teller to give him money. He handed the teller a blank sheet of paper with no instruction whatsoever, and the teller promptly filled the bag. When Messing returned the money, the teller was so blown away that he suffered a nonfatal heart attack.

In 1948, Messing traveled to Ashkhabad to perform, but when he got an eerie feeling about the city, he cancelled his performances and left. Three days later, an earthquake in Ashkhabad killed 50,000 people. Had he not made his prediction, it was pretty likely he would have been counted among the fatalities. Instead, Messing lived to a ripe old age, dying in 1974 at the age of seventy-five.

Ruth Montgomery
Automatic Writing
(1913–2001)

[Psychic Arthur Ford] convinced me that there was
something to this. He said that psychically he was
getting that I could do automatic writing. I did not

even know what that was. But he told me how to go
about it, how to hold the pencil. It always begins with
the pencil. And so, when this writing began, I
thought, 'What's going on here,' because I knew I
wasn't doing anything. I couldn't even let the pencil
go. It wasn't me who wrote.

> —Ruth Montgomery, explaining how she
> began automatic writing, in an April 2000
> interview with author Tatiana Elmanovich

How would the modern world react if at some time in the near future, a famed and serious female journalist, say, Paula Zahn, announced she would be retiring from journalism and only a couple of years later published a book she claimed was scribed in its entirety through a process called automatic writing—that a group of "spirit guides" had used her as a passageway through which to communicate their important messages from beyond? It's pretty darn likely that the laughter this generated might be so powerful as to cause the oft-predicted great shift of the earth on its axis in and of itself.

But when ultra respected Washington reporter Ruth Montgomery switched careers in just that way, in 1970, she, for the most part, was not only not scorned or ridiculed, but was embraced by those she knew, who began sharing their psychic experiences with her. The fact that she had come forth with her task didn't take away from her for those who knew her, rather, it legitimized for many a field that had been before left only to quacks and flakes.

Born in 1913 in southern Illinois, Ruth Montgomery grew up the prototypical midwestern, all-American girl. In fact, her ancestors had come to the New World from England and Germany as early as before the American Revolution.

When Ruth was still in high school, the family moved to Waco, Texas, where Ruth finished school and began her first career. Ruth always knew she wanted to be a reporter—of course, throughout her uneventful Christian upbringing, she could never have guessed what kind of reporter she was going to be remembered forever as being.

AP WORLDWIDE

An only child, her early years were essentially without paranormal event. Ruth had a psychic aunt, Charlotte Cunningham, but no one took her very seriously. As those who didn't believe what she accomplished later in life might think ironic, Ruth had no imaginary friends. She was a level-headed, fact-based journalist, through and through, and this was the stance she took until the day she died.

When Ruth was seventeen years old, she got her first job as a newspaper reporter in Waco and put herself through school. That job sparked a very successful first career, and she went to Washington, D.C., where she met her husband, Bob, and hit the big time.

In Ruth's time as a Washington columnist, she covered five presidencies, from Franklin Delano Roosevelt to Lyndon Johnson. She was even president of Roosevelt's White House Press Conference Association and later, president of the National Women's Press Club. Ruth was in impeccably good standing in Washington and was respected by the world at large, even attending frequent dinners at the White House.

Ruth's work encompassed more than just her column. She authored a book called *Hail to the Chiefs*. In fact, throughout her life, Ruth would author sixteen books; the last of which she wrote at age eighty-seven. One of her earlier books sparked an interest in psychic phenomena. In 1965, she wrote a best-selling book on one of the preeminent psychics of the time, Jeane Dixon (see page 86), called *A Gift of Prophecy*, which began to open her eyes to the possibility of psychic phenomena.

A couple of years later, Ruth was given an assignment to do a story on séances, which was to be a nationally syndicated seven- or eight-part series. In her research, she attended countless séances and was "read" by many mediums. The main thrust of her work was to disprove the phenomenon; she ended up getting more interested in it, if just casually.

And then she met psychic Arthur Ford.

Ford was in Washington while Ruth was working on her series, and Ruth met with and interviewed him. When she entered his hotel room, she immediately began to pull down shades and turn off the lights, a practice she had learned in the hundreds of séances she had attended, in which mediums needed to practice in the dark. A befuddled Ford came into the room and told her it wasn't necessary to work in the dark, that he could channel just fine in the light.

They sat together for hours. What he channeled for her really clinched it for Ruth. In her questioning, she remained coolly objective. And then he relayed for her a message from her father. Growing up, her father had never bought into a concept of the afterlife. So when the message that came through, from him, that he had been wrong and that he had been turned around, Ruth was hooked.

Ford gave her more information, and the more he told her, the more sense he made. A die-hard journalist was not going to allow herself to be easily swayed, however. But the pull was eventually too strong. As she reported in a later interview, "I made several long distance calls the next day and every single one of [Arthur's stories] proved to be absolutely true!"

Ruth was impressed by Ford. She made it a point to see him every time he was in town after their fateful meeting and the two began a friendship that would last to the end of his life—and beyond. Ford was equally impressed with Ruth, and believed from messages he had been receiving that she, too, had a psychic gift. Ford explained to Ruth that she had a talent for automatic writing and that she was to pursue it immediately. She was flattered by this, but, at least at first, didn't take him too seriously. Then another friend of Ruth's received the message in her dealings with automatic writing that Ruth could, in fact, do it and that it was time to try.

So one otherwise uneventful morning in 1968, Ruth Montgomery picked up a pencil, put it to paper, and after a brief time, began to scribble on a page. "It seemed as if a great hand put itself over my right hand, and the pencil began going wildly, heavily into circles and figure eights," she said. From that moment, her famed spirit "Guides" began to channel through her, and the rest is history.

At the time Ruth started to dabble in automatic writing, she was still covering her Washington beat and she didn't make that much out of it. For her, it was just a hobby and nothing more. In 1970, when her husband, Bob, retired, she gave up her column and the Montgomerys moved to Mexico.

Away from the pressures of Washington and what damage her gift might do to her reputation, she started to take her automatic writing more seriously.

Ruth eventually counted twelve Guides, but she never knew who they all were. They didn't make themselves known at first. When Arthur Ford died in 1971, however, he became one of them. Another one she knew for sure was someone known only as "Lily." She soon came to learn that Lily was actually a friend from a former life. He was a seventeenth-century monk, who had known Ruth in a previous life. There were about ten others, including, in time, her own father, and, after he passed, Bob.

Her dealings with the Guides was something essentially shared only among friends and the people closest to her, so when the

Guides advised her that it was time to pull all her writings together and make a book of it, she listened. Ruth's husband always supported her in whatever she wanted to do, and while he didn't particularly buy into her work, he didn't discourage her, either. Ruth's mother, however, was a different story. She was very wary about her daughter's new pastime and pleaded with her to not go through with publishing her work. "Ruth, please don't do that," she implored her daughter. "Presidents call you by your first name. They invite you to White House dinners, please don't humiliate yourself. They'll think you're a kook!"

Ruth decided the messages were much too powerful to hold back, so she compiled the writings into book form and shipped them off to her publisher. The first book of the Guides, *A Search for the Truth* (1967), was finally published. Ruth's mother's fears had to have been assuaged when not only did the book become a best seller, but it didn't tarnish Ruth's reputation at all. In fact, instead of being reviled and received with scorn, her former colleagues not only embraced it, but they even shared their experiences with her. "It was as if a damn had broken down and water was gushing out," Ruth said.

The general public was just as accepting, and Ruth constantly received letters from admirers explaining that "this is the first time I ever believed because I have been reading your column for years, and I know that you write truth and not fiction."

In explaining how automatic writing worked with her Guides, she said it was important to write at the same time every day. This was because, as the Guides explained to her, her spirit contacts will serve as gatekeeper and keep mischievous spirits out. Also interesting to note was that she never started the day with the Guides volunteering information; she had to get them started by asking a question. Ruth started this work in pencil; one day the Guides told her to switch to a typewriter. She tried a word processor, but it never did the trick.

The one condition she stipulated with her Guides was that they never manifest themselves in any way that would startle her. "I don't want to see you and I don't want to hear you," she told them. "This is my life now, but I will take your writing if you will leave me alone the rest of the time."

One of the most significant developments of Ruth's writing was the concept of "walk-ins." As she explained, "walk-ins were souls on the other side who had earned the right [in previous lifetimes] that if they wanted to, they could come in and replace a soul that is in desperate need of leaving the body . . . one who either does not want to maintain it, or who is dying and can't keep it alive. . . . The walk-out goes into the spirit the same as you and I will when we die."

Ruth's experiences with her spirit Guides may have challenged some of her early Christian beliefs, but, like Edgar Cayce (see page 61), a psychic she began to greatly admire, she was able to make peace with the contradictions.

But what also developed were clean-cut explanations for other contradictions, which could be tied up into tidy little boxes of meaning. For example, she could understand and even justify divorce by applying it to her understanding of walk-ins. One day, a person might find him- or herself all of a sudden married to another soul— that the soul of his or her spouse might "walk out" and be replaced with a stranger, as though one spouse feels out of place in the marriage and feels like he or she has woken up a different person one morning, living a completely wrong life, and the other, exasperated by the actions of the perceived "stranger" exclaims, "I just don't know who you are anymore!" She understood divorce now, and how most marriages never survive this.

Abortion is an issue even more controversial. Why can abortion be justified? Ruth said, "The Guides say, and also, Edgar Cayce said, that the soul enters at or around the time of birth, not at conception." And what about miscarriages and stillbirths? In these cases, a soul had decided it did not want to be born into a particular situation and thus did not occupy its assigned body. On a metaphysical level, a conceived child not being born is not a matter of sin or error, but redirection.

Perhaps the most unnerving information that the Guides passed through were predictions of potentially apocalyptic, cataclysmic events. One of these predictions, and the one most others are grounded on, is that soon the earth will shift on its axis, creating utter havoc on the planet. The south pole will move to the southern area of South America and the north pole will shift to somewhere in the Pacific Ocean. This will lead to climate changes, and places like New York City and Florida will vanish completely. "[The Guides] say that Earth is overdue for a cleansing," she explained.

Initially, the Guides, through Ruth, had predicted that this shift would take place around the turn of the twenty-first century. As Cayce had delivered very much the same message, Ruth was comfortable with the change. She explained that "about three or four years before the turn of the century they began telling me it would be postponed. . . . So now they're indicating it probably wouldn't be before 2012."

Throughout the chaos, it is predicted that a walk-in president will help the people of the world by telling them where to go and how to handle the "new world." Before her death, Ruth assured believers that this presidential walk-in will not be Bill Clinton, nor will it be the one that follows. Ruth didn't live to see the events of September 11, 2001; skeptics have diminished her work for not having predicted them.

Ruth and her husband, Bob, were happily married fifty-seven years. "I felt terrible when Bob died," she said about his passing. But as he continued to communicate with her, she was comforted by the fact that the dead "have not gone any place, they are still alive. And one thing that does for you is this: it makes you realize there is no such thing as death."

In her last interview in April 2000, Ruth said she was ready to join her friends on the other side. When she published her last book at age eighty-seven, she completed her mission on Earth and was "ready to go." She even picked up smoking again.

Ruth died on June 10, 2001, and remained humble about her messages even to her final days. "I don't take credit for any of this, or the beautiful philosophy," the infinitely objective Ruth said. "I'm just an ordinary college graduate."

Nostradamus

(a.k.a. Dr. Michel de Nostradame)

Prophet

(1503–1566)

I do not say, my son . . . that future, very distant things cannot be known by any reasonable creature: on the contrary, the intellectually minded person is well able to perceive things both present and far-off

> *[provided] that [these] are not too utterly occult or*
> *obscure. But the perfect appreciation of things cannot*
> *be acquired without that divine inspiration, given that*
> *all prophetic inspiration takes its prime moving*
> *principle (first) from God the creator, then from*
> *fortune and instinct.*
>
> —Nostradamus, written in a letter
> to his eldest son, Cesar

You don't have to know anything about the world of psychics to recognize the name "Nostradamus." Even in a book that doesn't rate them, he could easily be considered the most important, significant prophet of all time.

Especially during the crisis that affected the world after September 11, 2001, he became a household name, even hitting the best-seller lists and clinching several positions at that. The reason for this was a stanza in one of his quatrains, that was mangled, misinterpreted, and much maligned to scare people into believing the end was near, which we will look at in greater detail a little later.

More than a prophet of future doom, however, Nostradamus was a man of many talents. He lived the true modern definition of "Renaissance man"; which is kind of ironic, because he in fact lived during the Renaissance period.

Born December 14, 1503, in St. Remy de Provence, in southern France, Michel de Nostradame was part of a large family, with plenty of siblings. His father, Jaune, was a notary and merchant. The family was Jewish, but were forced to convert to Catholicism when Nostradamus was quite young because of the ever-present Inquisition.

As a boy, Michel was reportedly highly influenced by Jewish occult literature. In addition, he was intrigued by kabbalah and other ancient schools of thought. He was also pulled in by the New Testament, especially St. John's Revelations (see page 34), which may or may not have had a direct influence on his later writings.

Growing up, Michel learned several languages, and was well

versed in the disciplines of math, astronomy, and astrology from his grandfather, his mother's father, Jean.

When Michel was nineteen, he went away to school and earned a degree in liberal arts. He later attended the Medical Faculty of Montpellier to earn his doctorate. He was expelled in October 1529 for experiments he conducted in alchemy, but managed to talk his way back into reinstatement a few weeks later.

After graduating, he went into practice. The plague hit Europe hard at this time, and Dr. Nostradame made a name and reputation for himself by treating its victims. So proficient was he, in fact, that he became a known specialist and actually cured many of his patients.

In 1534, Michel married Henriette d'Encausse. They had two children and shared an idyllic life together. Happiness and good times abounded. And then the plague hit home. Literally. Tragically, the doctor with the magic touch could not save his own family; within months of infection, he lost both his wife and his children to the deadly menace.

This chain of events sent him into a deep depression, so he gave up his practice and opted instead to be a wanderer. To forget the pain of his recent past, he traveled throughout Italy and France for the next six years, picking up new trades and trying to move on.

In the late 1540s, he landed up in Salon de Croux, and decided it was time to settle down again. Within a couple of years, he met and married Anne Ponsarde Gemelle in Salon, and they had two sons and three daughters together.

Michel started to get focused on work again. In 1550, he published an academic work as "Nostradamus," thus changing his name on record forever. He wrote and published the world's first medical dictionary, *Traite des Fardmens*. In 1555, he wrote a famous cosmetics cookbook called *Treatise on Cosmetics and Conserves*. He was well regarded in the French court and ended up writing several more academic works on various topics, including astrology.

Then he discovered prophecy. Starting in 1555, Nostradamus began writing his timeless *Centuries* collection of quatrains; there would be ten *Centuries* in all.

In addition to his writing and continuing to practice medicine, Nostradamus became heavily involved in public and social projects, including the irrigation of the Plaine de la Crau. This irrigation system is still in place today, as well as the house he lived in with Anne and their children.

In 1556, he was summoned by Catherine de Medici, who, impressed by his talents, appointed him royal physician.

Nostradamus enjoyed close ties with the royal family, in spite of his prediction of the death of Henry II, which he had predicted and which had come to pass in 1559.

By June 1566, Nostradamus had become quite ill with gout and arthritis. He drew up his will, worked to finish his quatrains, and wrote letters explaining his work and his message to his son.

In these letters, he explained to Cesar that "although . . . I have used the word 'prophet,' I would not attribute to myself a title of such lofty sublimity for the present." Most significantly, he, well, predicted, that he might make people nuts with some of the things he said. "I have by dint of long calculation composed [these] books of prophecies, each containing 100 prophetic astronomical quatrains, which I have intentionally arranged a little obscurely," he wrote. "They contain perpetual predictions for [the period] from now until the year 3797. Which will possibly cause some people to raise their eyebrows on seeing such a long prognosis; [yet these] things shall take place and shall be known everywhere beneath the sphere of the moon—by which I mean throughout all the earth, my son. For if you live [to] the natural human age you shall see in the area of your own native clime and heaven [these] future events take place."

Cesar published the last of his father's books after his death.

On July 1, 1566, Nostradamus told a priest, "You will not find me alive at sunrise." And he was right. On the morning of July 2, Nostradamus was found dead in his room. He was buried in the Church of St. Laurent in Salon, but he has never been forgotten.

Hundreds of years after his death, followers are forever trying to find and force meaning to his cryptic messages. Some believe he predicted the rise of Napoléon Bonaparte, the French Revolution, the atom bomb, the Moon landing, and, a claim most psychics make, the assassination of John F. Kennedy.

It's up for great debate, however, that he had meant to predict any of these events. As he admitted to Cesar, the quatrains are open to interpretation, which means, at least in the present, people will see whatever they want to see in them. In one verse, Nostradamus uses the word "Hister." Those who think they have him all figured out swear that this is a reference to Adolf Hitler; skeptics are quick— and accurate—to point out that "Hister" is the Latin name for the Danube River. As Nostradamus used Latin terminology for many of his writings, it isn't far-fetched to assume he meant the latter.

In another misinterpretation, people "read" into one of the quatrains that the end of the world would be in August 1999. Scientists and skeptics, as well as believers defending the seemingly mispredicted day of doom, point out that the "powerful king" of which Nostradamus spoke in this famous quatrain was not God coming down for Judgment Day, but rather a solar eclipse, which had, indeed, occurred at that time.

The most controversy ever generated over a passage from Nostradamus was clarified by David Emery, Nostradamus.org, shortly after September 11, 2001, when the panic and confusion began. This passage, which blazed from e-mail inbox to inbox after the Twin Towers fell, was a hoax (and note that its attribution is many years after Nostradamus's death):

> In the City of God there will be a great thunder,
> Two brothers torn apart by Chaos, while the fortress endures,
>   the great leader will succumb
> The third big war will happen when the city is burning.
>
> —Nostradamus 1654

Also a hoax:

> On the 11 day of the 9 month that . . . two metal birds would crash into two tall statues . . . in the new city . . . and the world will end soon after.

And yet another one:

> Two steel birds will fall from the sky on the Metropolis.
> The sky will burn at forty-five degrees latitude. Fire approaches
>   the great new city.
> Immediately a huge, scattered flame leaps up. Within months,
>   rivers will flow with blood. The undead will roam earth for
>   a little time.

This is the real passage, as translated from the original French, and found on Nostradamus.org:

> The sky will burn at forty-five degrees latitude,
> Fire approaches the great new city
> Immediately a huge, scattered flame leaps up
> When they want to have verification from the Normans.

If that doesn't put Apocalypse-crazed minds at ease, perhaps this astute observation from Bernard Harder will: "Even recognized Nostradamus fans will find it difficult to call their idol to the witness stand on whether the world will end in 1999," he writes, "because the Nostradamus prophecies, after all, continue until the year 3797."

P

Eusapia Palladino
Medium
(1854–1918)

*I am filled with much confusion and regret that I
combated with so much persistence the possibility of
the facts called Spiritualistic.*

—Professor W.H.O. Lombroso, of his testing
of Eusapia Palladino

If Leslie Flint (see page 114) thought he was the most tested
medium of all time, he must have not known the story of Eusapia
Palladino, a sultry Italian sexpot of a medium who was probably
tested more vigorously than any other, before or since.

Palladino is remembered for performing astounding, unexplainable feats, but just as much, when she could not pull it off, for
faking it—and pretty poorly at that. Sometimes, to cover up the flub,
she would try to flirt her way to credibility. As it has been reported,
Eusapia was "liable on awakening from her trances to throw herself
into the arms of the nearest male sitter with unmistakable intent."

Eusapia was born into poverty and bad luck in 1854. Her family
lived in Minervo-Murge, near Bari, in the province of Puglia, Italy—
which is right at the heel of "the boot." When she was young,
Eusapia was orphaned. Her mother died in childbirth. Her father
raised her for 8 years, but then was killed by robbers.

With no family left, Eusapia essentially fended for herself. Therefore, school was not an option or even a consideration. She had to
find work or perish, so she eventually got a job as a domestic for a
family in Naples. It was there that she discovered the talent that
would make her famous.

Much like the entire world at this time, thanks to the 1848 contact with the spirit world by the Fox sisters (see page 120), the owners of the household were intrigued by spiritualism. As a result, there was always a séance going on in the house while Eusapia was in their employ. The young servant girl would watch the magical happenings at her masters' table from the wings, and she was also captivated by the prospect of communicating with the dead. She didn't realize that the strange occurrences happening in the house might just be her doing.

During one of the many séances, Eusapia's talent surfaced, and now her masters had an even better reason to keep the young waif around: revenue. Soon, people were coming from all over to attend the young medium's mind-blowing séances. It started out innocently enough, with raps and bangs, but soon enough, she was levitating and spirits began manifesting themselves—and sometimes in very strange ways.

And as believers flocked to her in droves, so, naturally, did skeptics. Soon, the leading scientific minds in Italy were coming to Naples to see the clairvoyant servant at work.

The investigations officially started in the late 1880s. A Professor Lombroso, a most outspoken skeptic, was her first tester on record. He came to Naples confident he could show the young "country" con artist up and that it would simply be an open-and-shut case of unsophisticated parlor tricks.

But after attending many séances, try as he could, he simply could not find any way to trip Eusapia up. Her performance was flawless. He decided that either she must be for real, or he wasn't as clever as he thought he was. He eventually admitted that he believed she must be authentic, but his skeptical nature caused him continued doubt. So he decided to seek out some bigger guns and called in reinforcements.

The next trials would happen in Milan: her testers this time included Lombroso and many respected academics to whom he had written to assist in the effort. The result was the same. All were stumped. They could not scientifically explain the levitations and spirit manifestations. So the investigations continued.

In 1893 and 1894, when Eusapia was about forty years old, she was tested by Dr. Ochorwitcz in Warsaw and Professor Richet on the tiny island Île Rubard, off the coast of France. Neither could prove her a fraud, but, like Lombroso, both felt that there was something about her that just didn't add up. For whatever reason, she simply could not be trusted.

Then the Sidgwicks got involved. Henry Sidgwick was one of the founders and the president of the Society for Psychical Research (SPR) at the time. Both Henry and Mrs. Sidgwick had been involved in intensive testing of spiritualism, even having tested Kate Fox (see page 120) in 1874. The results of most of their findings had been bleak: They wanted to believe, but just about everyone they tested was shown up as a fake in the end.

Henry nearly gave up testing altogether. Penning a letter to a friend in June 1878, he wrote, "I have not quite given up Spiritualism, but my investigation of it is a very dreary and disappointing chapter in my life." He wasn't entirely daunted, however. he did help found the SPR in 1882 after all.

Nearly twenty years after he thought he'd given up on formal testing for good, he learned about Eusapia Palladino. Henry was both intrigued and hopeful that she would confirm to him that belief in spiritualism was not a waste of time after all.

The unwillingly jaded Sidgwicks headed to France in the summer of 1895 to witness the workings of this Italian wonder whom no one could seem to disprove. Within a matter of days, they gave up, disgusted, claiming they had been able to pinpoint that her powers were not real and were due to a vaguely described trick.

For Eusapia, that was the beginning of the end of her psychic career. Her powers were already on the wane, which began to show more and more—almost embarrassingly so. After this series of tests, the nervous medium began faking it, and sloppily, with disastrous results.

Still, with all the ambiguity, many were still hard-pressed to believe—and many to disprove. Alan Gauld still readily admitted that "[n]ot all the phenomena which occurred could be explained on any such simple hypothesis." Specifically, he was talking about odd bumps that would actually manifest themselves on Eusapia's body. "There were, for instance," he observed, "the curious protuberances from Eusapia's body which some sitters occasionally observed."

Some skeptics-turned-believers also suspected sabotage. Many believed that the testers themselves may have set some situations up in which they perpetrated the fakery, that Eusapia wasn't involved, and that they "planted" things to make her look guilty.

In 1898, Eusapia was back in Paris enduring more exhaustive tests, with Professor Richet and others. He was still convinced she was genuine and never faltered on that belief. Others were not so grounded in their initial convictions.

In 1901–02 and 1906–07, more séances were conducted and scrutinized in Turin, Italy. More phenomena occurred. Professor Morselli was convinced it was real, writing "the great majority of manifestations that occur . . . are genuine manifestations."

Eusapia endured the whole shebang. She allowed the testers to stick her in a cabinet, with her hands and legs held down. While she could produce some curious supernatural specimens, it was clear that she was losing her powers.

In 1908, a series of eleven séances in Turin showed more deceit, but there also seemed to be the possibility of redemption. The levitations and manifestations for which she was famed were somehow back. She moved a table. She produced a spirit hand from thin air. Hereward Carrington noted, "It is almost impossible to conceive the elaborate apparatus that would be necessary to produce all the effects observed by us."

After the 1908 tests in Turin, the SPR reported that there "was not detected fraud in any one of 470 phenomena at eleven séances." More tests conducted in the United States in 1909, however, painted Eusapia in a not-too-flattering light. Those who believed her continued to believe; those who would not, including Harry Houdini, of course, did not, and, at this point, never would.

Eusapia Palladino died in 1918, amid so much controversy still as to whether she was for real or not.

R

Grigori Rasputin
(a.k.a. Grigori Yefimovich Novykh)
Mystic, Healer
(c. 1865/6–1916)

*I feel that I shall leave life before January 1. I wish
to make known to the Russian people . . . what
they must understand. If I am killed by common*

> *assassins . . . you, Tsar of Russia, having nothing to*
> *fear, remain on your throne and govern . . . and . . .*
> *will have nothing to fear for your children, they will*
> *reign for hundreds of years in Russia.*
>
> —Rasputin, in a letter to Tsar Nicholas II,
> 1916

Looking at history, we see that the message of this letter is not only abundantly clear, but also undeniably prescient. The House of Romanov was about to be torn to bits by the revolting Russian people; whether this was connected to the murder of Grigori Rasputin or not is cause for much debate.

Rasputin, who, when he came to St. Petersburg, was thought of as many things, including a German spy, was not much more than a lovably detestable Russian rogue among a court of less-obvious rogues.

He conducted himself a bit like Aleister Crowley (see page 69), but for Rasputin, the concept of living wickedly really was for a "greater good." He believed that he would get closer to God and to holiness by being as immoral as he could possibly be, that the immorality of his mortal life would free him of sin in his immortal manifestation.

To that end, he had countless sexual exploits, bagging all kinds of influential babes—whether royal or just plain wealthy—and despite the fact that he rarely bathed. On top of that, he was reputed to be a drunken sot.

So could he have been responsible, at least in part, for the revolution that brought down tsarist Russia? Would the Russian Revolution have happened if not for the influential Rasputin? It's not really known, nor could it ever fully be. What is known is that the monarchy was already corrupt; it was only a matter of time before it was going to implode.

Grigori Yefimovich Novyk was born in the mid-1860s, in a village called Pokrosvskoe, in Tiumen' Oblast in the Tyumen region of Siberia, near the Ural Mountains. It certainly did not seem likely while he was growing up that he would ever get within 100 feet of any tsar.

When Grigori was about eighteen years old, he became deeply involved in religion, nearly joining a monastery at Verkhoture. But fate had other things in store for the tall, lanky lad. After sampling the monastic lifestyle for about a year, he returned to his small village and decided to settle down and get married. He had several children with his wife, Praskovia Fyodorovna; but the settled-down life just wasn't for him. He stayed married but decided he needed to travel and seek out adventure.

In 1901, he left home to wander through Europe, making sporadic visits to check in with his abandoned brood. While on the road, he was making a name for himself as a "holy man." During the course of his travels, he developed his religious philosophy of "driving out sin with sin," and changed his name to Rasputin, which means "debauched one," a distinction that more than complemented his persona.

In 1905, he made his way to St. Petersburg, where he immediately fell in with the upper echelon of Russian society. The story goes that he was introduced to Princesses Anastasia and Militsa, who couldn't get enough of his stories and everything he could tell them about the occult.

Other society women were drawn to more than just his dark knowledge, as they put themselves into full service to him to help him—and themselves—drive out sin with sin.

Comfortable, Rasputin at last had found a place in which he could settle. He didn't summon his wife and kids to join him, however, though they visited him in St. Petersburg often.

Rasputin got his true "in" with the royal family through Anya Vyrubova, who was closely tied to the ruling Romanovs. In his capacity as a healer, he had saved her after a train wreck nearly claimed her life. She was in a coma and not given any chance to survive. Rasputin took to her bedside and determinedly grabbed her hand, concentrated, and chanted, "Annushka, Annushka, rise!" She opened her eyes, and while she remained a cripple for the rest of her days, she never forgot the magic of Rasputin's healing ability.

Anya spread the word to Tsarina Alexandra, whose son, Alekski, was a hemophiliac. Out of options, the tsarina was desperate to save the life of her son and the heir to the throne. Anya was so passionate about Rasputin's healing powers that Alexandra decided to invite him to the Romanov court and see what he could do.

When the child was healed, Rasputin immediately became a favorite of the Romanovs—and rumor has it that he was especially in Alexandra's favor, not just for saving her son, but for an illicit affair that may have taken place between them.

In 1912, young Alekski had another attack, which Rasputin miraculously healed via telegram. With that, he became a near-god of the court.

Soon, Rasputin's influence was felt far and wide, and he was completely untouchable as long as he stayed in the Romanovs' favor. Anyone opposed to Rasputin was sent away, or, it has been speculated, even killed.

As time went on, Rasputin became less than modest about the influence he had in the court, which annoyed more than a few members of the nobility, especially those who had begun losing patience with the tsar and tsarina.

Rumors circulated that Rasputin had "nonconsensual sin purging" with many women of the court. Some said he collected the hair of virgins. Others reported him abusing children, including the royal children. The tsar and tsarina were entranced by Rasputin: they punished anyone who made these kinds of allegations and only pulled Rasputin in closer to them.

The people, and especially the nobility, felt that Rasputin was having a very negative effect on the Romanovs, and especially on Tsarina Alexandra. Rasputin was so hated, that in 1914 he was nearly stabbed to death by a prostitute. He pulled through, if only to live a couple more years.

Even in 1916, at the time of his death, Rasputin remained loved by the Romanovs. He had simply fallen out of favor with everyone else—and especially since the country was in a black depression over the loss of lives in the Great War, and the people were angry at Nicholas for getting involved.

Not a stupid man by any means, Rasputin began to feel the threat to his life and could see the handwriting on the wall about the end of tsarist Russia. So he wrote a letter to Tsar Nicholas, quoted, in part, in the epigraph at the start of this section.

Rasputin's death rivals his life in its absolute remarkability. Think of those horror movies where the bad guys keep getting "killed"—and then keep getting up. That convention is no doubt inspired by the murder of Rasputin.

On a December night in 1916, Rasputin was invited by Vladimir Purishkevich, Grand Duke Dimitri Pavlovich, and Prince Felix Yusupov, under the guise of meeting Felix's wife. In all his salacious, unwashed studliness, Rasputin was determined to sleep with the beautiful princess, so he gleefully accepted the invite. Irina was the much-coveted niece of the tsar, and it was an offer he could not refuse. It didn't occur to him that seduction would not be in the cards.

While he waited for the luscious princess to arrive, Rasputin's hosts filled him with cakes and wine, all laced with cyanide. His hosts watched in wonder as Rasputin wolfed down cakes and swigged back the wine. At one point, Rasputin reportedly clutched his throat as his enemies looked on in anticipation, but, thinking he was just thirsty, he chugged another glass of wine—and that seemed to do the trick.

When all the poison did not take effect, plan B had to go into effect. Prince Felix had no choice but to shoot Rasputin dead, which he did—or so he thought. When he returned with the others to remove the corpse, they found Rasputin with no pulse. When they set out to move the body, Rasputin, who was not, in fact, dead yet, actually got up and began choking Yusupov.

Breaking from Rasputin's clutch, Felix, along with the others, ran like a scared child to get more help; when they returned with rein- forcements, Rasputin was gone. A few minutes later, Rasputin was found in the courtyard, dragging himself to the home of Alexandra and Nicholas, whom he planned to tell of his own murder, if he could live that long.

When Felix and his conspirators spotted Rasputin, they shot as much ammunition as was in their guns. When Rasputin stopped moving, they got closer, kicking and bludgeoning him with anything they could get their hands on.

Not entirely convinced that he was dead—or that he wouldn't have another resurrection—they decided to bind his body in ropes and toss it into a canal. When the body finally washed up, the ropes had been broken and Rasputin's lungs were filled with water. Just as his murderers had suspected, he still wasn't dead when he landed in the canal. He died trying to free himself.

That was 1916, the same year Rasputin wrote the letter to Nicholas with the prediction that his life was in danger, and that if he was killed by Nicholas's people the empire would fall. Ten weeks later, the Romanovs were overthrown; less than two years after Rasputin's death, the family was executed. The Russian Revolution had begun. So was Rasputin responsible or not? It all depends on what you believe.

S

Mother Shipton
(a.k.a. Ursula Sontheil)
Prophet
(1488–1561)

A carriage without a horse shall go.
Disaster fill the world with woe. . . .
Around the world men's thoughts will fly
Quick as the twinkling of an eye. . . .
Through towering hills men proud shall ride
No horse or ass move by his side;
Beneath the water, men shall walk,
Shall ride, shall sleep, shall talk;
In the air men shall be seen,
In white and black and even green.
    —Mother Shipton, from her Prophecies

However much weight you're willing to give the concept of prophecy, you might find yourself just a little impressed by the messages of Mother Shipton, a provincial woman who lived before the age of science and progress and who recorded the verse above.

That she could envision a world where people moved around in cars, not propelled by any external means, is remarkable to say the least. But that she foresaw that thoughts could fly around the world—as we understand now by phone, by fax, and, most appropriately, by e-mail—was an inconceivable notion for most of the modern world even fifteen years ago; that people could live on submarines, "beneath the water," where they "ride," "sleep," and "talk"; and that humans would be traveling in the skies is nothing short of astounding.

Before she was Mother Shipton, she was Ursula Sontheil, the unfortunate product of a naive single mother and a fast-talking rogue. Born in 1488 in Knaresborough, North Yorkshire, England, Ursula did not come into the world with many—if any—advantages. Forget her mother's unpure status. Forget the poverty she would live in. Forget all this for a moment and take a look at the image of this woman that exists on record today. Certainly, Ursula, who could have been the poster child for all Halloween "witch" decorations, wasn't going to get very far on her looks. And yet, she is remembered centuries after her death.

Legend has it that Ursula's unfortunate mama, Agatha, was an orphan. And on top of being seduced out of wedlock, she, too, would leave behind an orphan, dying just after the birth of her daughter. Ursula came into the world in a cave by the Nidd River. Today, the cave is named for her. In fact, even in the twenty-first century, more than 100,000 tourists visit her birthplace each year.

It's been said that there's nothing in the world that brings more despair than an ugly baby; Ursula, therefore, bred despair in every life she touched. No one wanted to take the ugly infant in, but eventually, some kind soul relented. That poor soul was going to regret her kindness soon enough. Even when Ursula was a baby, strange things began to occur around her; as she grew up, it just got worse.

In her foster home, furniture moved across the room and pottery flew about. If that wasn't enough, when Ursula was still a toddler, her foster mother came home and the front door was open. Fearing the worst, she flew to the room where the child was being kept, and, much to her horror, both the baby and the crib were missing. After hours of searching with neighbors, Ursula was found naked, and with her crib, in the chimney. And, oh, yeah—they were floating.

Ursula wasn't drowned or burned after this incident; her ever-patient foster mother dreamed of the day that a man would come and marry the unfortunate girl and take her off her hands. She figured this was a pipe dream at best, but one had to dream.

As the years went on, it seemed less and less likely that anyone would want to make Ursula his wife. There was no ugly-duckling-into-graceful-swan metamorphosis for her. It seemed that as she matured into adulthood, she only became more ugly. According to an account of her life on MysteriousBritain.com, Ursula had a nose "of inproportional length with many crooks and turnings," a crooked build, and unflatteringly enormous "goggling" eyes. The outlook was bleak.

But then in 1512, surprising everyone for villages over, Ursula married a carpenter, Toby Shipton. Some say she had put a spell on him, but whatever the case was, she landed herself a man. Progeny was not in the cards; however, prophecy soon would be.

Soon, Ursula began to make prophecies for the townsfolk, with an exceptional degree of accuracy. Soon, she came to be known as "Mother Shipton," and the moniker stuck.

As her legend grew, Mother Shipton began making prophecies outside of her village and the neighboring towns, and was sometimes very politically prophetic. Additionally, she was not ever one to hold back on bad news. If she saw it, she told it, and that was that.

- "When there is a Lord Mayor living in Minster-yard, let him beware of a stab" she predicted. Soon enough, a lord mayor did come to live in Minster-yard, and he was stabbed to death by muggers.

- "The northern line of Tweed; the maiden Queen shall next succeed." This was her prediction of Elizabeth I, who ascended the throne at age twenty-five and never married.

- *"Triumphant death rides London through."* This was how she predicted the plague.

And there was plenty more where these came from. It's hard to say how much of this is really true, however. She, like her near-contemporary, Nostradamus, had a tendency to write cryptically, with the messages embedded in riddles and the meanings, in many cases, open to interpretation.

One prophecy she made is right in line with other psychics' predictions: that the earth will experience a shift on its axis. "Waters shall flow where corn shall grow; Corn shall grow where waters doth flow," she writes. Those psychics who have prophesized the shift have said that water will run where land once was, and that where water is now, people will live and dwell on dry land.

Mother Shipton died in 1561, and she predicted her own death. Her tombstone, which has long since disappeared, is reported to have read:

> *Here lies she who never lied,*
> *Whose skill so often has been tried*
> *Her prophecies shall still survive*
> *And ever keep her name alive.*

Emanuel Swedenborg
Mystic, Seer
(1688–1772)

When the first rays of the rising sun of spiritual knowledge fell upon the earth, they illuminated the greatest human mind before they shed their light on lesser men. That mountain peak of mentality was this great religious reformer and clairvoyant medium, as little understood by his own followers as ever the Christ has been. In order to fully understand Swedenborg one would need to have a Swedenborg brain, and that is not met with once in a century.

—Arthur Conan Doyle, *The History of Spiritualism* (1926)

COURTESY OF THE SWEDENBORG FOUNDATION

Well respected in his time and beyond, Emanuel Swedenborg was a great scientist, thinker, and theologian. But his story doesn't end there: At the age of fifty-five, Swedenborg either had a spiritual epiphany or a psychotic meltdown. Naturally, the stance that one takes depends on belief. Those who believe him also believe that Swedenborg actually spoke with God, who told him the true meaning of the passages in the Bible. Swedenborg was so reputable, that in time, even the most opposed of Swedenborg's contemporaries eventually had no choice but to believe him. And, of course, others were known to twirl their index fingers around their ears when his name came up.

Crazy or not, Swedenborg published more than fifty books—before and after his epiphany/meltdown. He made remarkable contributions to both science and divinity. He was one of the creators of metallurgy; he knew that the cerebral cortex was the dominant section of the brain years before anyone studied the brain; he predicted atomic theory; and he developed the basis of modern molecular mechanics.

He also had many followers. It goes without saying at this point in our survey that Arthur Conan Doyle worshipped Swedenborg like a messiah. Also in the Swedenborg camp were Helen Keller and a great many writers, including Thomas Carlyle, William Blake, Johann Goethe, Ralph Waldo Emerson, and both Robert and Elizabeth Barrett Browning. But was he for real, or had his nut officially cracked?

Act One: A Man of the Physical World

Born in Stockholm in 1688 as Emanuel Swedberg, he was raised the second son in a Lutheran family swimming in an ocean of religion. His mother died when he was very young. His father was Bishop Jesper Swedberg, a strict Lutheran minister and writer of hymns. He was also chaplain to the Horse Guards of Charles XI, a professor of theology at Uppsala University, bishop of Skara, and a member of the Swedish Diet or House of Nobles. Surely, his father was a tough act to follow, but Emanuel certainly rose to the occasion.

A privileged youth afforded Emanuel a distinguished education and the opportunity to travel extensively, of which he took full advantage, visiting Holland, Germany, and England.

He had a special affinity for England, which he carried his entire life, even though he nearly got himself killed there. When the ship docked, passengers were ordered to stay aboard the vessel as there was rumor of plague and the authorities wanted to quarantine the possible sick. Being possessed of a curious and rebellious nature, Emanuel disobeyed the orders and left the ship, an offense for which he was nearly hanged, but his father's influence saved him.

From the ages of eleven to twenty-one, Emanuel attended Uppsala University, earning his Ph.D. at age twenty-two. Because he adored England, he decided to settle there between 1710 and 1713.

Back in Sweden in 1716, still in his twenties, he was offered a position as math professor but opted instead to become assessor of the Royal College of Mines in Sweden, appointed by Charles XII. While there, he published *Daedalus Hyperboreus*, Sweden's first medical journal, in 1716, and edited the publication between 1716 and 1718. In 1719, the Swedbergs were ennobled, and their last name was changed to "Swedenborg."

Swedenborg was a reputed expert in mine engineering, physics, astronomy, metallurgy, zoology, politics, economics—you name it. As a result, he published lots of scientific literature on a variety of topics from mathematics, to geology, to anatomy, to physiology, to chemistry and physics. He wrote everything in Latin, though his works have been translated into more than thirty-three languages.

On top of everything else, if it can be believed, Swedenborg was also an inventor. He boosted the shipping economy with several inventions, including a machine for working salt springs and a system for moving large boats overland.

In 1747, he was nominated for president of the Royal College of Mines, but by that time, he knew the time had come for him to resign and see what his life's next mission was to be.

(Now would be an excellent time to take a deep breath and a huge leap of faith.)

Act Two: "Voice" of God

On an October morning in Amsterdam, Swedenborg had a vision that changed his life. All of a sudden, he felt as though he was falling into a great abyss. He was rescued at the last moment when a hand grabbed him and pulled him out; it was the hand of Jesus. From that point on, he continued to have visions in which Jesus talked to him, and in which his now-deceased father would speak to him and encourage him to pursue his theological work.

In the ensuing visions, God directly told Swedenborg that the Bible was, indeed, His word and law, there was no doubt about that. But not in the way it had been erroneously interpreted. Apparently, the obvious interpretation was not what God had intended, and God had chosen Swedenborg to help Him get His message across.

So Swedenborg got to work putting "God's spin" on the scriptures, rewriting whole sections in the words God Himself had given him. His first published reinterpretation, the eight-volume *Arcana Celestia* (1749–56), redefined the meaning of the books of Genesis and Exodus. "Of the Lord's Divine mercy it has been granted me now for several years," he wrote, "to be constantly and uninterruptedly in company with spirits and angels, hearing them converse with each other, and conversing with them." Several more works followed. In these, in addition to revising the Bible, he gave vivid descriptions of all the various "heavens" and "hells."

In Swedenborg's teachings, there is no one destination for the spirit world; it exists as a series of concentric spheres, each with its own persons and purpose. Life in the spirit world is just as it is here—except better. The old, decrepit, and diseased are given their young and healthy selves back.

Swedenborg said that at the time of death, your true self emerges and that the life you've been living may be proven little more than an affected fallacy. So, in Swedenborg's universe, how one spends eternity is not based on who he or she may have pretended or wished to be, but on an actual, inherent nature that could not be controlled, nor could it be changed. What may have put minds at ease was that, with this teaching, he also took away most people's biggest fears of what happens in the hereafter.

He said that there was no actual place such as hell or demonic beings known as devils; rather, the greedy, malicious, and evil spin around on one of the concentric spheres together, there to torment each other forever. For the righteous, this was a kind of delicious justice. The good, noble, and pure go to heaven, which is more a state of expanded awareness, a paradise for a scientist and a philosopher, than anything else.

He summed up eternity by saying "throughout eternity, people stay the way they are insofar as their intention or strongest desire is concerned." In other words, spiritual desire is the ticket to heaven, and worldly desire will put you in hell. "People who are involved in physical desire cannot breathe in heaven. If a person is taken there, he draws each breath like someone hard pressed in a struggle. But people who are involved in heavenly desire breathe more freely and live more fully the farther into heaven they are."

According to Swedenborg, or, God as the case may be, just as there was no true "heaven" or "hell," so there was no true religion; there was no one pathway to God. All religions, apparently, were meant to serve God, and God accepted and embraced each and every effort. Religion, no matter which, was encouraged, as humans are incapable of achieving a heavenly nirvana alone; they need religion to get to God. Swedenborg also revealed that God openly rejected atonement and the concept of original sin.

In addition to his talks with God the Father, the Son, and the Holy Spirit, Swedenborg also made a lot of contact with angels. He described the main purpose of these ethereal beings as guiding people to the spirit world when it's time to pass from the natural world. He knew this for a fact because he actually watched it happen many times after people died.

Swedenborg didn't believe everything that came to him, however. Sometimes he suspected he was being tested or tricked:

When spirits begin to speak to man, care should be taken not to believe them, for most everything they say is made up by them, and they lie; so if we permitted them to relate what Heaven is, and how things are in Heaven, they would tell many falsehoods, and with such strong assertion that man would be astonished; wherefore it was not permitted me when spirits were speaking to have any belief in what they stated. They love to feign. Whatever may be the topic spoken of, they think they know it, and if man listens and believes, they insist, and in various ways deceive and seduce.

One of the most interesting elements of Swedenborg's philosophy was his idea about the union of marriage. He proclaimed that marriage is the only way to become a complete person. Swedenborg said that there were two elements of personhood: man was born "intellectual" and woman "affectional." The balance between the two is essential, as it is only together that one whole person can ever truly exist.

Not in the Bible or any religious teachings of any kind, Swedenborg firmly believed in the possibility of sex in heaven. He believed that after death, partners would reunite and celebrate their love in an explosion of pleasure. However, he also accepted that what worked in life may not work in the afterlife; once the mask is lifted and the true self revealed, someone might be incompatible with a spouse and have to find another.

His feeling about the importance of the institution of marriage is a strange and almost sad epiphany for a man who died, after a ripe long life rich in many fulfilling and significant experiences and accomplishments, a bachelor—though he had tried to get married twice.

As would be the future case with Ruth Montgomery (see page 175), who would find a whole new use for her writing talent other than journalism, Swedenborg was mostly not scoffed at or ostracized. In fact, even after his "epiphany," he remained a respected intellectual—although not everyone could swallow the horse pill he forced on them. Immanuel Kant had at one time publicly denounced the man and wanted him locked away for good. And yet, even Kant relented and accepted that if a mind like Swedenborg's could believe, than maybe, just maybe, it was all true.

Swedenborg died on March 29, 1772, in his beloved London. Soon after, a new religion, Swedenborgianism, sprung up, based on his ideas and ideals. The Church of the New Jerusalem, the venue through which his message and values would be perpetuated and nurtured after his death, was founded in 1778 in England and remains in existence even today. In 1810, a society was formed to publish Swedenborg's works in English. Between 1869 and 1870, lithographed copies of his original manuscripts were published in Sweden.

God and the legions of heavenly hosts are only a part of the visions he had, although they are the most prominent. Aside from watching spirits leave their bodies as they died, Swedenborg also had countless premonitions. For example, at a dinner party in Goteborg in July 1757, Swedenborg had a vision of a fire raging through Stockholm, which was about 300 miles away from where he was at the time. Also, in 1762 he went into a trance and described the assassination of Peter III, tsar of Russia.

Those who claim schizophrenia mashed the great mind of Swedenborg into mush cannot easily explain why Swedenborg's words are so concise, his message so clear, and his intent so deliberate. Interest in Swedenborg and his visions continues to run rampant even hundreds of years after his death.

V

James van Praagh

Clairvoyant, Medium

(1958/9–)

It's like a radio station. . . . I will actually tune into, if you will, a certain energy. A frequency of the person's voice. I'm hearing their voice. And by hearing that voice, I receive impressions. . . . And I get words in front of me. So it all depends on how the spirit is communicating and what I'm feeling. Sometimes it's right on. Sometimes the person doesn't understand it. And it's funny because I make money not knowing what I'm talking about.

—James van Praagh, in an interview
with Larry King, 2003

While many psychics in recent years have become household names, not many can boast having a television miniseries made about their life and work—and being played by Ted Danson at that. But medium-clairvoyant James van Praagh can. The movie, *Living with the Dead*, which ran on CBS in April 2002, was based on his work as a forensic psychic, but this is but one facet of van Praagh's vast career accomplishments.

Born in the late 1950s, van Praagh was raised Irish-Catholic in the quasi-suburban town of Bayside, Queens, New York, the youngest of four children. Throughout his childhood, he was fascinated by death—not by the process itself, but what happens to someone after he or she dies. What happens to his or her spirit?

Part of the reason for this was that his early years were drenched in Catholicism and thus, his first notion of spiritualism was shaped by eight years of Catholic school.

Van Praagh won't say he hated going to Mass altogether. He loved the spectacle of it—the music and the pageantry. It was really the gore that turned him off of Catholicism. The idea that the Host and wine were transformed into the "body and blood" of Christ and that he was then expected to ingest it was just plain disgusting to him.

Despite his disgust, he was still compelled by the prospect of life after death, and as this was the only way at this time he could learn more about that concept, he stuck with it. At age fourteen, he entered the seminary in Hyde Park, New York. If he became a priest, he rationalized, he could spend his life exploring the possibilities. At the time, he didn't realize there were other venues. It didn't take long for him to realize the priesthood was not the right path for him. He stayed for only one year.

Van Praagh's fascination with the afterlife actually was more than ghoulish curiosity. From a very young age, he had been having "visions" that could not be explained. "When I was a little boy," he told Larry King during an interview on *Larry King Live*, "I used to see spirits all the time. I'd see colors around people. I'd see forms."

When he was eight years old, he was already trying to pull it all together—why his visions did not always jive with what he was being taught in church and school. One night, he prayed for God to reveal himself, and an amazing thing happened. He watched in awe as a giant hand came through the ceiling in his bedroom, aglow with heavenly light.

At ten years old, he was cutting school, as he often did, and hanging out with some friends in the cemetery. There, he saw two kids playing. When he mentioned it to his friends, they thought he was crazy. They didn't see what he saw. Thinking that they might be right, van Praagh went over to the tombstone where the children, who had now disappeared, were playing and read the inscription. Shockingly, the grave was for twins—a boy and a girl—who had died when they were four years old.

So one of the things that was especially troubling to him was that he thought everyone saw the same things he did. He hasn't changed that belief, however. He maintains that if others got in touch with themselves, and then saw the universe outside themselves, they, too, would be clairvoyant. "I think everyone is an intuitive to a degree," he says. "For me it took seven years of meditation to produce it."

After his time in the seminary, he decided to switch to public school and attended the local high school. When he graduated, he decided to head west and went to college at San Francisco State University. There, he completed a degree in broadcasting and communications, a degree that, with all the television and radio he would be doing later on, he actually could make use of.

After graduation, he headed south to Los Angeles, a natural place to break into broadcasting. By this point, he had fully turned off Catholicism and was wholly turned on to the concept of spiritualism. It made sense to him. It jibed with his own experiences and beliefs. Still, he didn't know what his destiny would be. In fact, he only got involved in metaphysics after he attended a spiritualist gathering, where a medium told him in two years time, this is what he'd be doing.

She was right. He soon learned that he was "clairsentient, which simply means clear feeling," he explains on his Web site. "I feel the emotions and personalities of the deceased. I am also clairvoyant . . . the first is feeling, the second is seeing, very much like Whoopi Goldberg in the movie, *Ghost*."

Of course, it was very difficult for him to explain and prove any of this to his Catholic family. They didn't buy into it until he was on television. Once they accepted it, however, they divulged that other members of his family had also been psychic, including his maternal grandmother and grandfather and his paternal grandmother.

In addition to his television work and articles about him featured in magazines and newspapers, he is the author of several best-selling books.

In 1997, he published *Talking to Heaven*. In this, he talks about his experiences as a medium and encourages others to make room for spiritual exploration by looking into things like karma, in addition to the afterlife and spirit guides. Its success was followed in 1999 with *Reaching to Heaven*, a kind of guidebook designed for charting the soul as it passes into life from the spirit world, its experience in the physical world, its repassage into the spirit world, and then into reincarnation.

In 2000, he came out with *Healing Grief*, a book that encourages the bereaved to not focus on their loss, but to work through grief. His most recent book, *Looking Behind: A Teen's Guide to the Spiritual World*, was published in 2003. This book is van Praagh's attempt to talk to a younger audience, who may be, as he was, confused about life and death. According to various book sales lists, the book is doing well.

Van Praagh also believes himself to be a healer. He makes his diagnoses by "seeing" the energy in a person's body; when he sees that an organ or section is dark or blocked, he identifies the problem.

Like many mediums, van Praagh is a firm believer in reincarnation. He sees time spent on the spirit plane as a kind of "waiting room," a place where you essentially hang out until you're ready to go back. He writes, "In the higher realms everyone is on the same level of spiritual understanding, like a symphony of beings in tune with one another. For some this may mean a reunion with members of their earth family. For others it could mean meeting with former friends and lovers from previous incarnations."

So how does van Praagh see reincarnation as being something significant to the living? "You build on personality," he explains. "So you'll build on certain things. And for instance, in a past life, if you have a liking for something, and you come back this time, you might have the same liking. Or you've heard about people who go to a certain area of the world and they feel very familiar with that, because they've been there before."

Like any high-profile psychic, van Praagh has his share of detractors. Like they have with John Edward (see page 91), skeptics have accused him of cold reading—of hurling questions at his sitters until something sticks. As a result, he spends—or, as he feels, "wastes," a lot of time proving himself. "I don't mind skeptics as long as they're open-minded skeptics," he says. "Skepticism is one thing, cynicism is something else."

One of the reasons he gets criticized is that he can't always bring through a specific person, which he defended to Larry King, "Just because someone has a desire to speak to that one person doesn't mean they'll be there."

Also, like Edward, van Praagh says he's perennially skeptical—he was way back when, when his talents first started to surface, and he's skeptical now.

In 2003, van Praagh launched *Beyond*, a syndicated television show, which aired for one season but was not picked up for a second one. "Unfortunately, the marketplace was not as responsive to 'Beyond' as we had hoped to move forward for season two," explained Donna Harrison, Tribune Entertainment senior vice president of unscripted programming, to *Daily Variety* in January 2003.

Van Praagh was crushed, but he is irrepressible and hard to discourage. He continues to deliver his messages and help people cope with grief. He doesn't see people privately anymore. He prefers to work in group settings as the energy of an audience inspires him. He does make special exceptions from time to time, however. In 1998, after Sonny Bono was fatally injured in a skiing accident, Cher, Sonny's ex, allegedly hired van Praagh to help her communicate with Sonny. (Her daughter Chastity appeared on *Beyond* a few years later.)

Whether or not van Praagh always gets the messages coming through correctly, it's not the be-all and end-all for him. "If I convey recognizable evidence along with even a fraction of the loving energy behind the message," he says, "I consider the reading successful."

Sources

"ABC, Psychic Reunite Bakely Family." *Knight-Ridder/Tribune News Service*. April 30, 2002.

"A Conversation with . . . Dannion Brinkley." LightWorks.com.

Adalian, Joseph. "'Beyond' At Death's Doorstep." *Daily Variety*. January 6, 2003.

"Adviser to Queen Elizabeth 1." (review). *Library Journal*. February 1, 2001.

Alden, Andrew. "Geology of the Delphic Oracle." About.com.

"Aleister Crowley." Skepdic.com.

"Aleister Crowley, the Great Beast." ThelemicGoldenDawn.com.

"Aleister Crowley and the Golden Dawn." ThelemicGoldenDawn.com.

"Alessandro Cagliostro." Wikipedia.com.

Allen, Steve, and Joe Nickell. "Psychic Sleuth Dorothy Allison and the Jonbenet Ramsey Murder." CICAP, The Italian Committee for the Investigation of Claims on the Paranormal. Also, ValleySkeptic.com.

"A Man Sent from God." BibleBelievers.org.

AmazingKreskin.com.

"Andrew Jackson Davis." AstralResearch.org.

"Andrew Jackson Davis." FamousAmericans.org.

"Andrew Jackson Davis and His Wives." SpiritHistory.com.

"Apollonius of Tyanna." Livius.org.

"A Real-Life Dr. Doolittle." AnimalDiscovery.com. 2003.

Ascher-Walsh, Rebecca. "The Medium Is the Message." *Entertainment Weekly*. July 28, 1995.

Atchison, Bob. "Rasputin." *Alexander Palace: The Time Machine, Palace Biographies*. AlexanderPalace.org. 1995–2001.

Baker, George, and Walter Driscoll. "Gurdjieff in America: An Overview." BMRC.Berkeley.edu.

Baker, Robert A. "Psychic Sleuths: ESP and Sensational Cases." (book review). *Skeptical Inquirer*. May–June 1995.

Bald, Margaret. "Apocalypse Not Now." *World Press Review*. September 1999.

Barr, Stephen. "The Case of the Psychic Sleuth." *Good Housekeeping*. March 1997.

Barry, John, Michael Isikoff, Melinda Liu, Stryker McGuire, Mark Hosenball, Alison Langley, and Malcolm Beith. "Periscope." (interview). *Newsweek International*. August 5, 2002.

Baugher, Bob. "John Edward's 3.3-Second Disclaimer." *Skeptical Inquirer*. November–December 2002.

"Beatification of Fatima Children, Jacinta and Francisco." Ewtn.com. May 13, 2000.

Beatification of Fatima Children Jacinta and Francisco." Vatican Information Service. TheMirGroup.org.

Beyerstein, Dale. "Edgar Cayce: The 'Prophet' Who 'Slept' His Way to the Top." *Skeptical Inquirer*. January–February 1996.

"Biography of the Life of William Branham. "LivingWordBroadcast.org.

"Biography of Nostradamus." Nostradamus-Repository.org.

Blavatsky.net.

Boone, Lucille M. "Edgar Cayce: An American Prophet." (review). *Library Journal*. September 15, 2000.

Bradshaw, Robert I. "Elijah." © 1999 by Robert I. Bradshaw.

Brown, Adam. "Pope Believes Fatima Saved Him." Associated Press. May 13, 2000.

Brown, Michael. "The Incredible Story of Maria Esperanza." *Spirit Daily Online*. SpiritDaily.com. December 2002.

"Cagliostro, Alessandro, Conte." *The Columbia Encyclopedia*. 6th ed. Columbia University Press. 2000.

"Cagliostro, Alessandro, Count." Encyclopedia.org.

Carbone, Gina. "Psychic Mediums Spread Message of Life by Communicating with the Dead. "Seacoastonline.com.

Carley, George. "An Interview with Leslie Flint, Independent Direct Voice Medium." Noah's Ark Society.

Carnell, Brian. "John Edward's Cold Reading Gig." Skepticism.net. June 2, 2003.

"Cayce, Edgar." *The Columbia Encyclopedia*. 6th ed. Columbia University Press. 2000.

Chalfont, Pat. "Voices in the Dark." (review). PastLifeTimes.net.

"Children Who Saw a Vision." BBC.com.

Christian, Graham. "Heaven and Its Wonders and Hell, Drawn from Things Heard and Seen." (review). *Library Journal*. January 1, 2001.

Coleridge, Daniel R. "Pet Psychic Exposes Sordid Secrets." *TV Guide Magazine*. 2003.

Conroy, Ed. "Ruth Montgomery, May, 1996." Eclectic Viewpoint.com.

Cook, James. "Closing the Psychic Gap." *Forbes*. May 21, 1984.

Cooper, Ilene. "The Other Side and Back: A Psychic's Guide to Our World and Beyond." (review). *Booklist*. July 1999.

Cribbs, Cindy. "Voices of the Dead." NewTimes.org.

"Daniel Douglas Home." Atheism.about.com.

"Daniel Douglas Home." Mysteries.pwp.blueyonder.co.uk.

Dannion.com.

"Dannion Brinkley: The Longest Clinically Documented Near-Death Experience." The Institute for Afterlife Research.

Darroch, S. "The Birth of Spiritualism. The Story of the Fox Sisters." Pararesearchers.org. Para-Researchers of Ontario.

"Dee, John." *The Columbia Encyclopedia*. 6th ed. Columbia University Press. 2000.

"Dee, John." Occultopedia.com.

Deffinbaugh, Robert L. "Jonah: The Prodigal Prophet." Biblical Studies Press, bible.org. 1998.

"Delphic Oracle Was an Ancient Glue-Sniffer." *Science & Technology*. August 3, 2003.

"Diamond Necklace, the Affair of the." *The Columbia Encyclopedia*. 6th ed. Columbia University Press. 2000.

Dilworth, James. "Alessandro, Count di Cagliostro." TheMystica.com.

Doherty, Brian. "Do What I Wilt." (review). *Reason*. February 2001.

"Do What I Wilt." (review). *Publishers Weekly*. September 11, 2001.

"E. Palladino Physical Medium." Noah's Ark Society Online. *NAS Newsletter*. November–December 1996.

"Earth Prophecy—Dannion Brinkley." MM2000.nu.

"Edgar Cayce." Skepdic.com.

"Edgar Cayce (1877–1945)—'The Sleeping Prophet.'" Crystalinks.com.

Sources

EdgarCayce.org.

Egby, Robert. "What Really Happened: A Backgrounder on the Fox Sisters of Hydesville." National Spiritualist Association of Churches Online. December 2000.

"Elijah." Bible.org.

"Elizabeth Joyce Biography." New-Visions.com.

"Elizabeth Joyce Predictions." NTSkeptics.org.

"Elizabeth Joyce." *On Wall Street*. January 2000.

Elmanovich, Tatiana. "Interview with James van Praagh." Tanika.com. October 9, 1996.

————. "Ruth Montgomery: A Conversation in Naples, Florida, on April 2, 2000." Tanika.com.

"Emanuel Swedenborg." Kirjasto.sci.fi/Sweden.htm.

"Emanuel Swedenborg: The Trigger of Psychic Vision." Near-Death. com.

Emery, David. "Rumor Watch: Terrorist Attacks on U.S. Did Nostradamus Predict the Tragedy?" Nostradamus.org.

"Enter the Psychic." Crime Library Online.

"Eusapia Palladino; Sir William Barrett, FRS." The International Survivalist Society. SurvivalAfterDeath.com. 2002.

"Falsehoods in Great Controversy Exposed: Rappings and Spiritualism." Ellen White.org.

Farha, Bryan. "Sylvia Browne: Psychic Guru or Quack?" Quackwatch. com. Fatima.org.

"Fatima Children." BlueArmy.com.

"Fatima's Third Secret Overshadows Historic Beatification of Two Children." ChristianityToday.com.

"Fatima's 'Third Secret' Revealed." BBC.com.

Figes, Orlando. "Rasputin." *The Great War and the Shaping of the 20th Century*. PBS.org.

Flanagan, Margaret. "McCalman, Iain. *The Last Alchemist: The Seven Extraordinary Lives of Count Cagliostro, Eighteenth-Century Enchanter*." (review). *Booklist*. June 1, 2003.

"Fox Sisters." *The Columbia Encyclopedia*. 6th ed. Columbia University Press. 2000.

Freedman, David Noel. "Biblical Prophets." LightPlanet.com.

Freier, Steve, and Nancy Freier. "A Conversation with Ruth Montgomery, 'Herald of the New Age.'" (interview). *The Inner Voice Magazine*.

Gage, Cynthia. "Plugged in with Dannion Brinkley." AtlantisRising. com.

Gates, David. "*Madame Blavatsky's Baboon*." (review). *Newsweek*. February 20, 1995.

"George Ivanovitch Gurdjieff." Gurdjieff-legacy.org.

GeorgeAnderson.com.

Gliatto, Tom. "Medium Rare: Skeptics Howl, But TV Psychic John Edward Says He Hears Dead People." *People Weekly*. May 6, 2002.

Gouk, Penelope. "John Dee's Conversations with Angels; Cabala, Alchemy, and the End of Nature." (review). *The English Historical Review*. June 2001.

Griffeth, Bill. "Interview with John Edward." *The Americas Intelligence Wire*. February 28, 2003.

"Grigory Rasputin." *The Fresh Guide to St. Petersburg*. Yusopov Palace Online.

Grossman, Wendy. "Lawsuits May Silence Critics of the Paranormal." *New Scientist*. July 13, 1991.

"Gurdjieff, George Ivanovitch." *The Columbia Encyclopedia*. 6th ed. Columbia University Press. 2000

"Gurdjieff, George Ivanovich." Occultopedia.com.

Hale, John R., Jelle Zellinga de Boer, Jeffrey P. Chanton, and Henry A. Spiller. "Questioning the Delphic Oracle: When Science Meets Religion at This Ancient Greek Site, the Two Turn out to Be on Better Terms Than Scholars Had Originally Thought." *Scientific American*. August 2003.

Hamilton-Parker, Craig. "The Psychics and the Celebrities: The Story of Craig and Jane Hamilton-Parker's TV Work." Psychic-Mediums.com.

———. "The Psychic Family Where Even the Pets Are Psychic." *The Daily Mail*. September 19, 1997.

———. "What Is Psychic?" Psychics.co.uk.

Harkness, Deborah E. "Shows in the Showstone: A Theater of Alchemy and Apocalypse in the Angel Conversations of John Dee (1527–1608/9)." *Renaissance Quarterly*. Winter 1996.

Harris, Tom. "How Nostradamus Works." HowStuffWorks.com.

Hart, Eloise. "The Delphic Oracle." TheSociety.org.

"Helena Petrovna Blavatsky." Crystalinks.com.

"Helena Petrovna Blavatsky." Fst.org.

Hodges, Ann. "Polly Doesn't Want a Cracker. Sonya Fitzpatrick Should Know: She's the Pet Psychic." HoustonChronicle.com.2002.

"Home, Daniel Douglas." *The Columbia Encyclopedia*. 6th ed. Columbia University Press. 2000.

Hommerding, Leroy. "The Esoteric World of Madame Blavatsky: Insights into the Life of a Modern Sphinx." (review). *Library Journal*. April 15, 2001.

Hughes, Dennis. "Interview with James van Praagh: Renowned Psychic, Spiritual Healer, Author, and Teacher." ShareGuide.com.

Hyman, Ray. "Historical Truth Is Not Exempt from Scientific Standards." *Skeptical Inquirer*. May–June 1995.

"Interview with James van Praagh." *The Americas Intelligence Wire*. January 10, 2003.

"Interview with Jane Hamilton-Parker, Craig Hamilton-Parker, Louise Reid-Carr." *The America's Intelligence Wire*. March 8, 2003.

"Intuitive Messengers: John Holland." ThePlanet.com.

"Isaiah." HistoryChannel.com.

Jackson, Lillian A. "The New Medium on the Block." *Electronic Media*. May 27, 2002.

Jackson, Wayne. "Jeane Dixon and the Psychic Hall of Fame." Christian Courier Online. April 17, 2000.

"James van Praagh." Who2.com.

"James van Praagh Is the Medium of the Moment." *Knight-Ridder/Tribune News Service*. June 8, 1998.

Jaroff, Leon. "Talking to the Dead: To Reach Those Who Have 'Crossed Over,' John Edward May Have Crossed One Line Too Many." *Time*. March 5, 2001.

Jay, Peter A. "*Madame Blavatsky's Baboon: A History of the Mystics, Mediums, and Misfits Who Brought Spiritualism to America*." (review). *Insight on the News*. April 24, 1995.

"Jeane Dixon." Wikipedia.org.

"Jeane Dixon: Jeremiah or Joke?" GoodbyeMag.com. January 1997.

"Jeane Dixon: A Modern-Day Prophet from Washington, USA." Euro-Tongil.org.

"Jeane Dixon and Prophecy." Equip.org.

JohnDee.org.

"John Edward." ESPministries.com.

"John Edward." TeenPeople.com. March 1, 2002.

"John Edward: Psychic Phenomenon." *People Weekly*. December 31, 2001.

"JohnEdward.net.

"John Holland." Eomega.org.

JohnHolland.com.

Johnston, S. Laurence. "Edgar Cayce's Vision: The Golden Touch." *Paraplegia News*. November 2000.

Kaufman, Joanne. "Medium Rare: British Psychic Phenomenon Rosemary Altea Makes a Good Living Talking to People Who Aren't." *People Weekly*. October 23, 1995.

Keathley, J. Hampton. "Hosea the Prophet." bible.org.

Kenner, Hugh. "*Madame Blavatsky's Baboon: A History of the Mystics, Mediums, and Misfits Who Brought Spiritualism to America.* (review). *National Review*. May 1, 1995.

Kim, Dr. Young Oon. "Emanuel Swedenborg." Euro-Tongil.org.

Kuntzman, Gersh. "Nostradamus, Move Over!" *Newsweek*. November 5, 2001.

"Ladies of the Rope: Gurdjiieff's Special Left Bank Women's Group." (review). *Publishers Weekly*. September 21, 1998.

LeslieFlint.com.

"Life on the Other Side: A Psychic's Tour of the Afterlife." (review). *Publishers Weekly*. June 19, 2000.

"M. Crandon Physical Medium: The Mediumship of Margery Crandon." Noah's Ark Society Online. 1998.

"Magic and the Occult of Britain: Mother Shipton." Mysterious Britain.com

Maione, Ian C. "Testing 'Put to the Test.'" *Skeptical Inquirer*. May–June 1998.

"Margery the Medium." PsychicInvestigator.com.

"Maria Esperanza." Betania.com.

"Maria Esperanza." Crystalinks.com.

Martin, Douglas. "Dorothy Allison, 74, 'Psychic Detective' Consulted by Police." *New York Times*. December 20, 1999.

Martin, James. "*Saved by the Light*." (review). *America*. October 22, 1994.

Mayles, Daisy, and Dick Donahue. "Past and Future Tenses." *Publishers Weekly*. July 23, 2001.

McNeil, Rob. "Diana Having Fun in Afterlife." *Evening Standard*. March 10, 2003.

Meoli, Daria. "He's Got Your Number." (The Amazing Kreskin). *New Jersey Monthly*. February 2003.

"Mina 'Margery' Crandon." Fst.org.

"Miracle Attributed to Dead Fatima Children: Young Siblings Will Be Saints: Dead Pair Credited with Healing Woman." *Detroit Free Press*. July 29, 1999.

"Modern Spiritualism: The Fox Sisters and the 'Rochester Rappings.'" *Rochester Regional Library Online*. 2000.

Montgomery Clifford, Mary. "Cyberweave: Spirituality and the Internet." August 2003.

Moore, Dennis. "Animal Planet Pulling in the Viewers." *USA Today*. 2003.

Morelli, Emily. "Dream on, Says Sylvia Browne." *Bookpage*. August 2002.

Morris, Holly J. "But Can She Curse in Kangaroo?" *U.S. News and World Report*. June 24, 2002.

"Mother Shipton's Complete Prophecy." *Nexus Magazine*. February–March 1995.

MotherShipton.co.uk.

New-Visions.com (Elizabeth Joyce's Web Site).

Nicholls, David J. "The Mediumship of Helen Duncan." Noah's Ark Society Online. noahsarksoc.co.uk.

Nickell, Joe. "John Edward: Hustling the Bereaved." CSICOP.org.

———. "'Psychic Detective' Dorothy Allison Dies." *Skeptical Inquirer*. March 2000.

"Nostradamus." Skepdic.com.

Nostradamus.com.

"Our Lady of Betania." MedjugorjeUSA.com.

"Pet Peeves: TV's Animal Psychic Sonya Fitzpatrick Says She Knows What's Bugging Our Beasts—Because They Tell Her." *People Weekly*. July 8, 2002.

"Peter Hurkos." Entertainment.msn.com.

"Peter Hurkos Biography." StephanieHurkos.com.

Peters, Kathryn M. "A Conversation with Dannion Brinkley." InLight Times.com.

Phillips, Kyra. "Interview with the Amazing Kreskin." *The Americas Intelligence Wire*. July 8, 2003.

Polidoro, Massimo. "The Search for Margery." *Skeptical Inquirer*. November–December 2002.

——, and Gian Marco Rinaldi. "Eusapia Palladino's Sapient Foot: A New Reconsideration of the Fielding Report." The Italian Committee for the Investigation of Claims on the Paranormal. CICAP.org. 2003.

"Pope Blesses Fatima Children." BBC.com. May 13, 2000.

Posner, Gary P. "The Incredible Gall of 'The Amazing Kreskin.'" *Tampa Bay Skeptics Report*. Spring 1992.

"Prophets and Prophecy." *Judiasm 101*. JewFaq.org.

Prose, Francine. "Proud Spirit." (review). *People Weekly*. June 30, 1997.

"Psychic Jeane Dixon Dies." Personal Freedom Outreach Online (pfo.org).

"Psychic Jeane Dixon Dies: 'Astrologer to Stars' Had Legions of Believers." CNN Interactive. CNN.com. January 26, 1997.

Pursell, Chris. "'Crossing Over' Sensing Skeptics." *Electronic Media*. March 5, 2001.

Radford, Benjamin. "John Edward's Televised Tragedy Séance Scrapped." *Skeptical Inquirer*. January–February 2002.

"Rah Rah, Rasputin: Rapsutin Gets Shot and Poisoned and Keeps on Tickin'." History House. CNN.com.

Ramsland, Katherine. "Seeing the Future?" CrimeLibrary.com © 2002 Courtroom Television Network LLC.

Randi, James. "I was Brilling: Sylvia Browne, John Edward, the Maharishi Mahesh Yogi, Bad Astronomy, and More." *Skeptic*. Summer 2002.

——. "John Edward and the Art of Cold Reading." *Skeptic*. Summer 2000.

"Rasputin." Channel14.com.

"Rasputin: Poet. Magician. Healer. Prophet. Holy Monk." It.stlaw.edu.

Roach, John. "Delphic Oracle's Lips May Have Been Loosened by Gas Vapors." *National Geographic News*. National Geographic.com. August 14, 2001.

RosemaryAltea.com.

"Ruth Montgomery." NearDeath.com.

Scully, James. "Saved by the Light: The True Story of a Man Who Died Twice and the Profound Revelations He Received." (review). *National Reveiw*. September 12, 1994.

Sheaffer, Robert. "The Year the World Would End, and Other Prognostications." *Skeptical Inquirer*. March–April 1995.

Shermer, Michael. "Deconstructing the Dead: Cross over One Last Time to Expose Medium John Edward." Skepdic.com.

"Should We Believe Nostradamus?" *Africa News Service*. September 27, 2001.

"Some People Have Successfully Foreseen the Future." Near-Death.com.

"Sonya Fitzpatrick, the Pet Psychic." SpiritSite.com

SonyaFitzpatrick.com.

"Special Profile on John Holland." OfSpirit.com.

Stashower, Daniel. "The Medium and the Magician." *American History*. 1999.

Stasi, Linda. "Critter-Cal Condition." *New York Post*. 2002.

Stefanidakis, Rev. Simeon. "Forerunners to Modern Spiritualism: Andrew Jackson Davis (1826–1910)." First Spiritual Temple Online. Fst.org.

———. "Forerunners to Modern Spiritualism: Emanuel Swedenborg." First Spiritual Temple Online. Fst.org.

Steinhaus, Rochelle. "Visions of Death: Can Psychics 'See' What Detectives Cannot?" Court TV.com © 2002 Courtroom Television Network LLC.

Steward, Russell. "Famous Psychic People." Kajama.com.

"Swedenborg, Emanuel." *Benet's Reader's Encyclopedia*. 3rd ed. 1987.

"Swedenborg, Emanuel." *The Columbia Encyclopedia*. 6th ed. Columbia University Press. 2000.

"Swedenborg, Emanuel." *Merriman-Webster's Biographical Dictionary*. May 1995.

Swedenborg.com.

Sylvia.org.

"Talking to Animals with Sonya Fitzpatrick." WashingtonPost.com. 2002.

Taylor, Troy. "The Fox Sisters: The Rise and Fall of Spiritualism's Founders." PrairieGhosts.com. 2003.

Taylor, Troy. "The Strange Case of 'Margery': The Mystery of Houdini's Greatest Nemesis." PrairieGhosts.com. 2003.

"Text of the Third Fatima Secret." BBC.com.

"The Aleister Crowley Foundation." ThelemicGoldenDawn.com.

"The Amazing Kreskin." American Entertainment International, Inc.

"The Amazing Kreskin." Who2.com.

"The Final Secret of Fatima." ABCnews.com.

"The Fourth Way Made Simple." EsotericLinks.com.

"The Fox Sisters." AnOpenDoor.com.

"The Fox Sisters." First Spiritualist Temple Online. Fst.org. 2001.

"The Fox Sisters and the Spiritualism Movement." The Church of the Living Truth Online. LivingTruth.net. 1999.

"The Mediumship of Leslie Flint." Noah's Ark Society Online.

"The Nightclub Psychic." Crime Library Online.

"The Oracle at Delphi." PsychicInvestigator.com

"The Psychical Mediumship of D.D. Manning." Noah's Ark Society Online.

"The Premise and Promise of Fatima." Special Fatima Issue. May 11–14, 2000. CatholicDoors.com, DailyCatholic.org.

"The Sorcerer of Kings: The Case of Daniel Douglas Home and William Crookes." (book review). *Publishers Weekly*. November 1, 1993.

"The Story of the Prophet Jonah." Pearls of Wisdom Online. Pearls.com.

"The Talented Mr. Cagliostro: Ian Thomson Reviews the Seven Ordeals of Count Cagliostro." Telegraph.co.uk.

"The Teachings of 'the Prophet' William Branham." LetUsReason.org.

"The Truth about Nostradamus." *Asia Africa Intelligence Wire*. February 15, 2003.

"The World's Most Mysterious Man: Edgar Cayce's NDES and Revelations." Near-Death.com.

"The Youth of Apollonius." AlchemyLab.com, TheMystica.com.

"This Day in Church History: Pope Celebrates 'Special Bond' in Fatima." Cbc.ca. May 15, 2000.

"Tomb Reader: A Man of Grave Expectations Celeb Psychic John Edward Talks to the Dead, But not Everyone's Buying His Brand of Good Grief." *Entertainment Weekly*. September 14, 2001.

Underdown, James. "They See Dead People—or Do They?" *Skeptical Inquirer*. September–October 2003.

"Uri Geller." Skepdic.com.

"Uri Geller Libel Suit Dismissed." CSICOP.com. August 1994.

UriGeller.com.

VanPraagh.com.

"Voices in the Dark." (review). SpiritCommunicator.com.

Walker, Alexander. "Leslie Flint." Cheroki.com.

Washington, Ramona. "Pet Psychic Talks to Local Animals." News-Sun.com. 1999.

"We Got Male: John Edward." *Redbook*. April 2003.

Weeks, Byron, and Christopher Goodheart. "Ruth Montgomery's Remarkable 1979 Earth Changes Prophecies." November 27, 1999.

"What Fatima's Third Secret Taught Us." AmericanCatholic.org. © 1996–2003 St. Anthony Messenger Press.

"What Fatima's Third Secret Taught Us." AmericanCatholic.org. August 2000.

"Who Was Daniel Home?" Spartechsoftware.com.

"William Branham: 'A Prophet of Notable Signs and Wonders.'" ChristianHistory.org.

Wolf, Buck. "The Fault Lies Not in Our Stars." ABC News Online. abcnews.com.

———. "Uri Geller: Litigious Psychic." ABC News Online. abcnews.com.

"Wolf Messing." Wikipedia.com.

"Wolf Messing." WorldOfTheStrange.com.

Wood, Gail. "Uri Geller: Magician or Mystic?" (review). *Library Journal*. September 15, 1999.

"World Survives the End, Nostradamus Wrong Again." *Skeptic*. Summer 1999.

"You Own the Power: Stories and Exercises to Inspire and Unleash the Forces Within." (review). *Publishers Weekly*. December 6, 1999.

"You'd Think van Praagh Would Know." *Broadcasting & Cable*. January 13, 2003.